99 Ancient Secrets
and Mysteries
of the Bible Explored

museum of the Bible

BOOKS

Executive Editorial Team
Allen Quine
Wayne Hastings
Jeana Ledbetter
Byron Williamson

Developmental Editor
Dr. Tim Dailey
Len Woods

Managing Editor
Christopher D. Hudson

Senior Editors
Mary Larsen
Jennifer Stair

Worthy Editorial
Kyle Olund
Leeanna Nelson

Design & Page Layout
Mark Wainwright,
Symbology Creative

Cover Design
Matt Smartt,
Smartt Guys design

Cover Art
"Jonah Leaving the Whale"
Oak, 37.7 x 55.6 cm. Inv.
1887 by Brueghel, Jan the
Elder / bpk Bildagentur /
Alte Pinakothek, Bayerische
Staatsgemaeldesammlungen,
Munich, Germany / Art
Resource, NY

99 Ancient Secrets and Mysteries of the Bible Explored
© 2017 Museum of the Bible, Inc.
Published by Worthy Publishing Group, a division of Worthy Media, Inc. in
association with Museum of the Bible.

ISBN-10: 1945470097
ISBN-13: 978-1945470097

Library of Congress Control Number: 2017949576

Unless otherwise indicated, Scripture quotations are from the ESV®
Bible (The Holy Bible, English Standard Version®), copyright © 2001
by Crossway, a publishing ministry of Good News Publishers. Used by
permission. All rights reserved.

Scripture quotations marked NRSV are taken from the New Revised
Standard Version Bible, copyright © 1989 the Division of Christian
Education of the National Council of the Churches of Christ in the United
States of America. Used by permission. All rights reserved.

Scripture quotations marked (NIV) are taken from the Holy Bible, New
International Version®, NIV®. Copyright © 1973, 1978, 1984, 2011 by Biblica,
Inc.™ Used by permission of Zondervan. All rights reserved worldwide. The
"NIV" and "New International Version" are trademarks registered in the
United States Patent and Trademark Office by Biblica, Inc.™

Scripture quotations marked NLT are taken from the Holy Bible, New Living
Translation, copyright © 1996, 2004, 2007, 2013, 2015 by Tyndale House
Foundation. Used by permission of Tyndale House Publishers, Inc., Carol
Stream, Illinois 60188. All rights reserved.

Scripture quotations marked JPS are taken from The Holy Scriptures
According to the Masoretic Text, a New Translation. Jewish Publication
Society, 1917.

Scripture quotations marked KJV are taken from the King James Version,
1611. Public domain.

Scripture quotations marked NASB are taken from the New American
Standard Bible®, copyright © 1960, 1962,1963, 1968, 1971, 1972, 1973, 1975,
1977, 1995 by The Lockman Foundation. Used by permission.

Scripture quotations marked NKJV are taken from the New King James
Version®, copyright © 1982 by Thomas Nelson. Used by permission. All
rights reserved.

Produced with the assistance of Hudson Bible.

Printed in the USA.

1 2 3 4 5 6 7 8 9 LBM 22 21 20 19 18 17

BIBLE PLACES • Todd Bolen/BiblePlaces
17,61 • A.D. Riddle/BiblePlaces 35 • MM/
BiblePlaces 42 **COMMONS.WIKIMEDIA** • 27,
29, 30, 32, 38, 39, 40, 43, 44, 45, 49, 50, 58, 61,
64, 67, 73, 82, 83, 88, 95, 98, 99, 101, 102, 106,1
07 **DOVER IMAGES** 70, 72, 75, 85, 89, 91, 93,
105, 109 **GOOD SALT** • 84 **ISTOCKPHOTO**
• Andrew_Mayovskyy/Istockphoto: 111 • assalve/
Istockphoto: 111 • bauhaus1000/Istockphoto:
33vboygovideo/Istockphoto: 26 • duncan1890/
Istockphoto: 104 • earthmandala/Istockphoto:
76 • EvanTravels/Istockphoto: 37 • ivan-
96/Istockphoto: 52 • lbllama/Istockphoto:
16 • Meinzahn/Istockphoto: 45 • RudolfT/
Istockphoto: 77 • sedmak/Istockphoto: 18
• stevenallan/Istockphoto: 62 • TerryJLawrence/
Istockphoto: 23 • traveler1116/Istockphoto: 16
• vvvita/Istockphoto: 65 • Walt41/Istockphoto: 77
• WitR/Istockphoto: 33 • wynnter/Istockphoto:
83 • ZU_09/Istockphoto: 21 **SHUTTERSTOCK**
• AG-PHOTOS/Shutterstock: 88 • alefbet/
Shutterstock: 20 • Aleksandar Todorovic/
Shutterstock: 68 • Alexey Stiop/Shutterstock: 53
• Alla Khananashvili/Shutterstock: 67 • Anibal
Trejo/Shutterstock: 11 • Authentic travel/
Shutterstock: 32 • Baimieng/Shutterstock:
48 • Borna_Mirahmadian/Shutterstock: 39
• Bykofoto/Shutterstock: 81 • Cris Foto/
Shutterstock: 43 • Diego Barbieri/Shutterstock:
96 • Dmitry Petrenko/Shutterstock: 22
• eFesenko/Shutterstock: 95 • Elena Mirage/
Shutterstock: 28 • Eric Isselee/Shutterstock: 10
• Esteban De Armas/Shutterstock: 19 • Eunika
Sopotnicka/Shutterstock: 63,10 • Everett - Art/
Shutterstock: 8, 31, 42, 108 • Heather Shimmin/
Shutterstock: 90 • IndianSummer/Shutterstock:
46 • jorisvo/Shutterstock: 14, 92 • Jukka Palm/
Shutterstock: 107 • kerenby/Shutterstock:
25 • Kwiatek7/Shutterstock: 22 • Lagui/
Shutterstock: 94 • Lerner Vadim/Shutterstock:
60 • mandritoiu/Shutterstock: 35 • Marben/
Shutterstock: 30 • Martchan/Shutterstock:
9 • mbolina/Shutterstock: 20 • MehmetO/
Shutterstock: 13 • Miguel Nicolaevsky/
Shutterstock: 48 • MstudioG/Shutterstock: 102
• Nejron Photo/Shutterstock: 12 • Nickolay
Vinokurov/Shutterstock: 17 • Nicku/Shutterstock:
57 • Oleg Ivanov IL/Shutterstock: 54 • paul
prescott/Shutterstock: 69 • Peter Hermes
Furian/Shutterstock: 9 • Peter Popov Cpp/
Shutterstock: 34 • photostockam/Shutterstock:
13 • pio3/Shutterstock: 15,100 • ProfStocker/
Shutterstock: 27 • Renata Sedmakova/
Shutterstock: 24, 28, 34, 47, 51, 57, 79, 81, 86, 97,
103 • Robert Hoetink/Shutterstock: 59 • ruskpp/
Shutterstock: 10, 38 • S1001/Shutterstock: 110
• Shutterstock: 106 • slavapolo/Shutterstock:
95 • Valery Rokhin/Shutterstock: 101 • volkova
natalia/Shutterstock: 68,78 • vvoe/Shutterstock:
66 • Willyam Bradberry/Shutterstock: 49
• yousang/Shutterstock: 6 • Zvonimir Atletic/
Shutterstock: 41, 90

museum of the Bible
BOOKS

WORTHY®
PUBLISHING

99 Ancient Secrets and Mysteries of the Bible Explored

Introduction

In reading the Bible or hearing stories from the Bible, have you ever had questions like *Whatever happened to the garden of Eden? Is there actual evidence for Noah's ark? How did the walls of Jericho "come a tumblin' down"? Where is Jesus's tomb?*

If so, you are not alone. The Bible's eye-popping stories often leave out just enough details to make us wonder, *What really happened here?* And our human curiosity nags at us just enough to make us want to pursue the answers. Perhaps the mysteries within the Bible are the primary reason it remains the best-selling book of all time.

99 Ancient Secrets and Mysteries of the Bible Explored focuses on the most puzzling biblical claims and stories—unprecedented acts of nature, inexplicable acts of destruction, unusual creatures, bizarre people, and cryptic prophecies. In these pages, we'll examine these perplexing enigmas by looking briefly at pertinent historical, cultural, archaeological, and grammatical details. Is there evidence for incredible accounts such as the destruction of Sodom and Gomorrah or the conquest of Canaan? How do we make sense of intriguing biblical characters such as the mysterious Melchizedek, a talking donkey, or the wise men who follow a star?

The riveting photos, maps, stories, and rich details from the Bible that are included in *99 Ancient Secrets and Mysteries of the Bible Explored* will help you engage the Bible like never before.

CHAPTER ONE

In the Beginning

01 Divine Pronouns

The Bible begins at the beginning, with the story of creation. In the opening sentences we read: "And God said, 'Let there be light,' and there was light. God saw that the light was good, and he separated the light from the darkness" (Genesis 1:3–4, NIV).

Did you catch that? *He* separated light from darkness. The Bible's writers used masculine pronouns to refer to God—not just here in the opening lines of the Bible, but all the way through.

Some people see this and wonder, "Isn't that sexist? Is the Bible actually saying that God is *male*?"

Several details from the Bible are worth considering:

- Those who continue reading in Genesis 1 quickly come to a verse that says, "God created mankind in his own image, *in the image of God he created them; male and female he created them*" (Genesis 1:27, NIV, emphasis added). A possible conclusion here is that it requires both sexes, male and female, to properly reflect what God is like.

- The Torah expressly forbade the people of Israel from making any sort of male or female idol or god (Deuteronomy 4:15–16).

- Though God is typically referred to in the Bible as a Father (Matthew 6:9) or a King (Psalm 24:10), other biblical metaphors depict God using explicitly feminine descriptions. For example, God is likened to a woman in childbirth (Isaiah 42:14) and to a mom who nurses (Isaiah 49:15) and comforts her children (Isaiah 66:12–13). God is even said to be like a momma bear robbed of her cubs (Hosea 13:8) and a mother hen gathering her chicks (Matthew 23:37).

Authors of the Bible's books lived in male-dominated eras and cultures, a factor that may heavily contribute to the sexist tone of the biblical writing. But there's no denying they included both male and female descriptors to teach about the nature of God. ∎

Above: *The Fall of Man* (1616) by Hendrik Goltzius (1558–1617).

O2 The Lost Rivers of Eden

According to Genesis 2:10, a river flowed from the garden of Eden and divided into four headstreams. Those who see Eden as historical and not mythical have long felt that accurately identifying these rivers could possibly lead to the discovery of the site of this biblical paradise.

There is little question about two of the rivers mentioned in the text: the Tigris and Euphrates. Both exist today, located in Iraq and Iran. Some scholars have suggested the Karun River in southwestern Iran might be the biblical Gihon. Evidence has recently come to light regarding the potential location of the other river said to flow out of Eden: the Pishon. According to Genesis 2:11, the Pishon River flows in the "land of Havilah, where there is gold."

Satellite photography confirms the presence of an underground river running below a dry riverbed that empties into the Persian Gulf. This subterranean river extends to the mountains of Hejaz, located in Saudi Arabia. Intriguingly, gold has been mined in this area, known as Mahd adh-Dhahab, since ancient times. Is this Havilah? If this underground river is indeed the ancient Pishon, could it conceivably lead to the location of the primordial garden paradise?

Some speculate that these four rivers converge underneath the headwaters of the Persian Gulf. If this is true, then those seeking evidence for the garden of Genesis 1–3 will need deep-sea diving equipment to confirm it. ∎

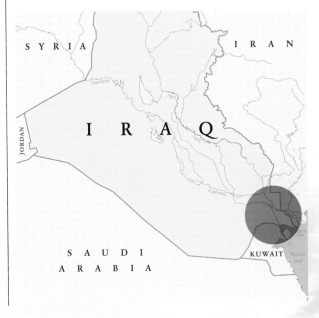

Below: Euphrates River in Syria near Dura Europos.

03 A Talking Serpent

In the Genesis account, Adam and Eve's idyllic existence in Eden is interrupted by a talking serpent.

The serpent makes its appearance in Genesis 3:1: "Now the serpent was more subtle than any beast of the field which the LORD God had made" (JPS). Different translations of the Hebrew Bible use other words to describe the serpent: "crafty" (NIV), "cunning" (NKJV), "shrewdest" (NLT).

Who or what is this creature? Many Bible scholars assume the serpent was a snake because in many Near East cultures evil and chaos often were symbolized by the figure of a snake. However, the evidence is inconclusive. Others suspect the serpent was a dragon, like Tiamat, the goddess of primeval waters, in the Babylonian story *Enuma Elish*. The biblical account in Genesis 3 doesn't specify.

How do we explain the serpent's ability to talk? The Jewish philosopher Philo (25 BC–AD 50) claimed that "in olden times . . . [a] snake could speak with a man's voice" (*On Creation* 156). The historian Josephus wrote, "At that time all living things spoke the same language" (*Jewish Antiquities* 1:41).

Though the serpent is a central figure in the garden story, it mysteriously slithers in and out of the story. This creature continues to attract the attention of biblical interpreters, prompting questions about what kind of "beast of the field" it may have been. ■

04 What Happened to the Garden of Eden?

Throughout the ages readers of the Bible have speculated about the location of the garden of Eden.

Genesis 2:14 references the well-known Tigris and Euphrates Rivers. These actual waterways prompted some medieval mapmakers to suggest possible sites.

However, Genesis 3:24, in describing the expulsion of Adam and Eve from Eden, speaks of a divine effort to keep anyone from reentering this ancient garden. That passage reads: "After [God] drove the man out, he placed on the east side of the Garden of Eden cherubim and a flaming sword flashing back and forth to guard the way to the tree of life" (Genesis 3:24, NIV). The word *cherubim* is the plural form of *angel*. In other words, the biblical text seems to suggest that God did not want this site found and/or reinhabited.

Here's something else to consider: Genesis 6–8 tells the story of a great flood. The cataclysmic event described in those chapters would have buried billions of things in rock layers all over the earth. As a matter of fact, the Middle East contains hundreds of feet of sediment strata, indicating water once covered the region. Could the original site of the garden of Eden lie forever hidden somewhere deep underneath these strata? ■

Above: *Expulsion of Adam and Eve from Paradise* by Gustave Doré (1832–1883).

O5 In Those Days There Were Giants

Genesis offers a mysterious glimpse of a group of creatures called "the Nephilim" that existed before the Flood: "The Nephilim were in the earth in those days, and also after that, when the sons of God came in unto the daughters of men, and they bore children to them; the same were the mighty men that were of old, the men of renown" (6:4, JPS).

Nephilim is not an ethnic designation. It comes from a Hebrew verb that means "to fall" or "to be cast down."

For this reason, some have proposed that this verse is suggesting that the writer of Genesis viewed the Nephilim as fallen angels in human form.

Following the flood story, Numbers 13:32–33 identifies the Nephilim as "descendants of Anak" (NIV) and inhabitants of the land of Canaan. They are described as people "of great size" (NIV).

The ancient Greeks told stories of giants, describing them as human creatures who lived and died—and whose bones could be found coming out of the ground where they had been buried long before. Indeed, large humanlike bones can be found today in Greece. From Paul Bunyan of American folklore to the Norse creator-god *Ymir*, humanlike giants populate the stories of many civilizations.

Were these Nephilim the last remnants of a race of giants or the exaggerated imagination of ten frightened Israelite spies? According to Numbers 14:1–35, the Israelites believed the spies' account of these "giants" and were too afraid to follow God's command to enter Canaan. What exactly were the Nephilim? We may never know. ◼

And they told him, "We came to the land to which you sent us. It flows with milk and honey, and this is its fruit. However, the people who dwell in the land are strong, and the cities are fortified and very large. And besides, we saw the descendants of Anak there."

NUMBERS 13:27–28

Above: *The Fountain of the Fallen Angel,* Buen Retiro Park in Madrid, Spain.

O6 Noah's Great Construction Project

Many scholars, intrigued by the biblical account of Noah's ark, have sought to get their minds around such an ancient, giant construction project. Genesis 6:15 gives the ark's dimensions as 450 feet long, 75 feet wide, and 45 feet high—or 300 cubits long, 50 cubits wide, and 30 cubits high (a cubit is about eighteen inches). Maritime experts, by the way, say this six-to-one length-to-width ratio is considered ideal. These dimensions would provide excellent stability for the vessel on the open sea.

These measurements give a volume of 1,518,000 cubic feet. This means the ark would have had a capacity equal to 569 modern-day railroad cars. In a word, the ark was gargantuan, which prompts the question: How could one man—Noah—complete such a massive construction project?

Genesis 5 tells us that Noah had three sons. Also, Noah's father, Lamech, and grandfather, Methuselah, were still alive during most of the years leading up to the Flood. Perhaps they—and others—helped. However, when the Flood finally came, only eight people—Noah, his wife, their three sons, and their wives—boarded the ark (Genesis 7:13).

We have countless other questions: What specific tools did Noah use? How did he cut and join the pieces of lumber? How did he build the necessary scaffolding?

Genesis gives very few specifics about this epic project. It simply says that Noah "found favor with the LORD" (Genesis 6:8, NLT) and "did everything exactly as God had commanded him" (Genesis 6:22, NLT). ∎

07 Ararat's Secret

Noah's ark, according to Genesis 8:4, "came to rest on the mountains of Ararat." The biblical Mount Ararat is believed by some to be a volcanic peak in the region bordering Turkey, Iran, and Armenia.

Throughout history there have been numerous reports of large boatlike objects on Mount Ararat. The earliest references, dating to the third century BC, suggest the ark was still clearly visible on the mountain.

In the past century aerial photographs of unusual structures on the mountain, reports of visits to the ark, and even claims of recoveries of wooden timbers from the ark have excited those who have sought to find the remains of this ancient artifact. It has been theorized that the mountain's snow and ice recede sufficiently for the ark to be seen only during exceptionally warm summers. However, most Bible scholars suggest that in the years following the Flood, the ark was likely scavenged for building materials or it deteriorated with the passage of time.

Because Mount Ararat is located in a sensitive border region, Turkey often refuses requests to investigate the area. Yet it is possible that the search will expand to other peaks in the Ararat range as efforts continue in the hunt for evidence of the biblical account of the most calamitous event ever to occur on the planet. ∎

The fountains of the deep and the windows of the heavens were closed, the rain from the heavens was restrained, and the waters receded from the earth continually. At the end of 150 days the waters had abated, and in the seventh month, on the seventeenth day of the month, the ark came to rest on the mountains of Ararat.

GENESIS 8:2–4

Above Right: Khor Virap Monastery with Mount Ararat in the background.
Above Left: A biblically inspired rendition of Noah's ark on Mount Ararat.

08 A Tower Reaching the Heavens

The fertile land of southern Mesopotamia is the backdrop for the mysterious story of the tower of Babel. The tower's construction is suggested to be the reason why so many different languages are spoken in the world today.

Before Babel, "the whole earth had one language and the same words. And as people migrated from the east, they found a plain in the land of Shinar and settled there" (Genesis 11:1–2). Then they concocted a grandiose scheme: "Come, let us build ourselves a city and a tower with its top in the heavens . . . lest we be dispersed over the face of the whole earth" (Genesis 11:4).

Archaeologists suspect this tower was actually a ziggurat: a pyramid-like structure prominent throughout ancient civilizations. We see such ancient structures at sites like Machu Picchu in southern Peru, Puma Punku and Tiahuanaco in western Bolivia, the Moai statues on Easter Island in the South Pacific, and Gobekli Tepe in Turkey.

Ziggurats were typically dedicated to a civilization's patron deities. They were believed to serve as stairways from heaven to earth so that the gods could come down and bring blessing to their subjects. There is no archaeological evidence that people ever used these structures. They were built for the gods (which could explain why the author of Genesis would portray God as frowning on such activity).

The real mystery is how these architectural marvels were built at all. ■

Above: *Tower of Babel* (1563) by Pieter Bruegel the Elder (ca. 1525–1569).

CHAPTER TWO

The Patriarchs

Stained glass window depicting Abraham, Słupsk, Poland.

$\bigcirc 9$ Who Is This Satan?

A number of Bible scholars agree that the book of Job likely depicts events that occurred during the patriarchal period of biblical history (ca. 1900 BC). If that's true, then one of the oldest stories of the Hebrew Bible contains the most detailed glimpse of the infamous character called "Satan" (*Ha-Satan* in Hebrew means "the accuser") .

In this ancient book, Satan appears before God along with other "members of the heavenly court" (Job 1:6, NLT). When God points out Job's faithfulness to God, Satan, in keeping with his name, acts like a prosecuting attorney. He alleges that Job's devotion is tied to God's favor to Job. This charge prompts a divine wager. With God's permission, Satan is allowed to bring calamity into Job's life. Satan is convinced that Job will curse God if his blessings are stripped away.

This supernatural being becomes known by many other names in later Jewish tradition (Belial, Samael). He is well known in the New Testament as the "devil" (*diabolos*, the Greek translation of *Satan*; Matthew 4:1), the "evil one" (Matthew 6:13), the "adversary" (1 Peter 5:8), and the ruler of a host of rebellious angelic beings (Matthew 25:41).

The Gospels show Jesus being personally tempted by Satan (Matthew 4; Mark 1; Luke 4). In the Gospel of John, Jesus calls him the "father of lies" and a "murderer from the beginning" (8:44, NLT). Because of this designation, and because Satan is so often described with the imagery of a serpent and dragon (see Revelation 12), many Bible interpreters assert that it was  this angelic adversary who, in the form of a serpent, originally tempted Adam and Eve in the garden of Eden. ∎

Be sober-minded; be watchful. Your adversary the devil prowls around like a roaring lion, seeking someone to devour.

1 PETER 5:8

Above: *Jesus and Satan*, illustration.

10 Ur of the Chaldeans

Genesis tells us that Abraham's father, Terah, took Abraham (then called "Abram"), Abraham's wife, Sarai, and his grandson Lot "from Ur of the Chaldeans to go into the land of Canaan" (11:31).

Many archaeologists identify Ur with modern-day Tell el-Muqayyar, located approximately 220 miles southeast of Baghdad. Excavations of the site from 1922 to 1934 by English archaeologist Charles Leonard Woolley revealed that Ur, a city of enormous size and opulence, was the crown of ancient Mesopotamian civilization. Located near the Persian Gulf, it was an important trade center.

The most valuable discovery of Woolley's excavations was the royal cemetery, with its sixteen large tombs containing jewelry, gold artifacts, wheeled vehicles, and the remains of the bodies of the kings of Ur and their attendants.

Archaeologists estimate that during the time of Abraham there were approximately 24,000 people living in the city of Ur. They lived in relative comfort and worshiped many gods, with their chief god being Nanna, the moon god.

With climate change and land misuse, the population of Ur dwindled. People began migrating either to northern Mesopotamia or south toward the land of Canaan. When the Persian Gulf receded farther and farther south from the city, Ur lost its economic clout and eventually fell into ruin around 450 BC. ■

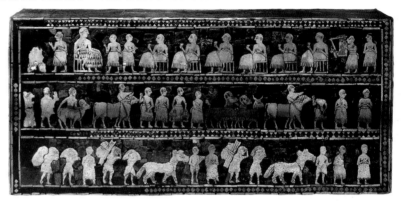

11 The Destruction of Sodom and Gomorrah

In Genesis 19:24 we read that "the LORD rained on Sodom and Gomorrah sulfur and fire." According to the biblical text, Abraham looked in the direction of the two cities and "saw the smoke of the land going up like the smoke of a furnace" (Genesis 19:28, NRSV). The description is suggestive of a kiln-like furnace or smelting forge.

Scientists and archaeologists have researched at length to shed light on the nature of this type of cataclysmic destruction.

As for the location of these cities, scholars have focused on two ancient sites bordering the southern Dead Sea: Bab edh-Dhra and Numeira. Excavations have uncovered evidence that these places were destroyed by an immense conflagration. But what could have brought about such devastation? The answer to this mystery may be found at the bottom of the Dead Sea, one of the most unique geological regions on the planet.

Geologists have long suspected the presence of petroleum-based substances and flammable gases trapped deep underneath the Dead Sea. If ignited, these volatile materials could very well have precipitated a massive explosion followed by destructive fires.

Another factor may explain how the cities were destroyed: Both archaeological sites are located on a major fault line extending along the eastern side of the Dead Sea. It is possible that a strong earthquake could have triggered the fiery devastation that consumed Sodom and Gomorrah. ■

Above: Standard of Ur from Ur Royal Cemetery, 2600 BC.   Right: The Dead Sea coastline.

12 Abraham: A Father's Sacrifice

13 Mysterious Melchizedek

It's unthinkable to us, but child sacrifice was a part of some ancient, primitive religions. Archaeologists have found evidence of such practices among Phoenician, Arabian, Incan, Mayan, and Aztec cultures. Parents sacrificed their children in gruesome rituals—all in the hopes of appeasing divine wrath, currying divine favor, or demonstrating extreme religious devotion.

According to Deuteronomy 12:31, the people of Israel were strictly forbidden from engaging in the child sacrifice practices of the people in and around ancient Canaan: "You shall not worship the LORD your God in that way, for every abominable thing that the LORD hates they have done for their gods, for they even burn their sons and their daughters in the fire to their gods."

Given this clear prohibition, what are we to make of the stomach-turning story from Genesis 22 in which God himself commands Abraham to offer his son Isaac as a sacrifice? It seems like a giant contradiction.

This mystery is solved, many scholars assert, in the climax of the story. They point out God's intervention at the last second. He stops Abraham from carrying out this grisly act, and instead supplies a wild ram for the sacrifice. In other words, they argue, the God of the Hebrews was demonstrating in this dramatic moment that he is nothing like the Canaanite deities. He not only doesn't require such barbaric offerings but also forbids them (see Leviticus 18:21, 20:3). ∎

The Hebrew patriarch Abraham had an extraordinary encounter with someone named Melchizedek, described as both "king of Salem" and a "priest of God Most High" (Genesis 14:18). Melchizedek offered bread and wine to Abraham and blessed him. Abraham in turn paid a tenth of all his goods to acknowledge Melchizedek's status. Who is this king of Salem who commanded the reverence of Abraham?

Melchizedek is widely considered one of the most enigmatic of biblical figures. He abruptly shows up in this story. Just as quickly, he disappears from the Hebrew Bible narrative.

This name pops up again in Psalm 110—a prophetic song ascribed to David. The opening verse of this psalm was later quoted by Jesus (Luke 20:42). The idea of this psalm is that Israel's coming Messiah-King would, like the ancient Melchizedek, also function as a priest and would have victory over the nations.

And Melchizedek king of Salem brought out bread and wine. (He was priest of God Most High.) And he blessed him and said,
"Blessed be Abram by God Most High,
*   Possessor of heaven and earth;*
and blessed be God Most High,
*   who has delivered your enemies into your hand!"*
And Abram gave him a tenth of everything.
GENESIS 14:18–20

The mystery of Melchizedek's identity deepens when we understand that his name means "king of righteousness" and his title "king of Salem" means "king of peace." In the New Testament, Melchizedek is described as "without father or mother or genealogy, having neither beginning of days nor end of life, but resembling the Son of God he continues a priest forever" (Hebrews 7:3).

Melchizedek is even mentioned in literature found at Qumran. He is described as a divinely empowered judge, a supernatural deliverer, and the one who awards inheritance to the righteous.

Much mystery surrounds Melchizedek, but this much is clear: the Bible writers considered him remarkable. ∎

Above: *Abraham and Isaac* (1713) by Giovanni Battista Pittoni (1687–1767), San Francesco della Vigna, Venice, Italy.

When King Solomon finished building the temple, he placed the revered ark of the covenant "in the inner sanctuary . . . the Most Holy Place" (1 Kings 8:6–8), where the high priest entered just once each year. Centuries later, when the Babylonians invaded Jerusalem in 586 BC, the ark was lost to history. Many scholars suspect it was probably destroyed when the First Temple was destroyed. But, as demonstrated by the popular *Raiders of the Lost Ark* movie, interest in this mysterious relic continues to the present day.

Since the fate of the ark of the covenant is unclear, some biblical researchers admit it might possibly be hidden in a vast cave system under the ancient temple site. Others suggest it may be near Qumran by the Dead Sea. Other theories have the ark buried in various locations in Europe, South Africa, and even the United States. Meanwhile, the Ethiopian Orthodox Church claims to have it in their possession!

Another intriguing possibility is found in the book of 2 Maccabees, a book of Jewish history written in Greek around the first century BC. The author describes how the prophet Jeremiah escaped Jerusalem ahead of the Babylonians and hid the ark of the covenant in a cave on Mount Nebo in Jordan. There it will supposedly remain until the day when "God gathers his people together again and shows his mercy" (2:7, NRSV). ■

Computer generated representation of the Ark of the Covenant.

15 The Behemoth of Job

The book of Job contains the following divine description of a fearsome creature that lives in or near water: "Behold, Behemoth, which I made as I made you; he eats grass like an ox. Behold, his strength in his loins, and his power in the muscles of his belly. He makes his tail stiff like a cedar; the sinews of his thighs are knit together. His bones are tubes of bronze, his limbs like bars of iron" (40:15–18).

The reference to the behemoth's "tail stiff like a cedar" causes some Bible scholars to suggest that a crocodile is being described here, a view supported by Job 40:23, which describes the behemoth as a water animal: "Indeed the river may rage, yet he is not disturbed; he is confident, though the Jordan gushes into his mouth" (NKJV).

Since, however, the crocodile does not eat "grass like an ox," an alternate hypothesis arose that the behemoth is none other than a hippopotamus. Although a hippo can give the impression of serenity—"He lies under the lotus trees, in a covert of reeds and marsh" (Job 40:21, NKJV)—it is an immensely powerful and dangerous animal.

Interestingly, ancient hippopotamus bones have been discovered at different locations in Israel, lending credence to the theory that this two-ton mammal was the behemoth. ∎

Above: The banks of the Jordan River, Israel.

CHAPTER THREE
___

The Exodus

Israel's Exodus from Egypt (1880), wood engraving.

An Israelite House in Egypt

Why can't we find more Egyptian records documenting the presence of the Israelites in Egypt? This may be due to a common practice of many ancient court historians to portray the ruler in the most favorable light. Given this custom, one would hardly expect to find ample records of the humiliating loss of Pharaoh's army while pursuing his former workforce during the Exodus.

Even so, archaeologists are convinced they have discovered clear evidence of an Israelite presence among the ruins of Thebes, the ancient capital of Upper Egypt.

Ancient peoples tended to have "trademark" styles of building. By examining the floor plan of an excavated structure, along with the pottery connected with it, archaeologists can often determine who constructed a dwelling and inhabited it and when.

One distinctive style of a four-room house was so common in the central hill country of Canaan that modern-day archaeologists refer to it as the "Israelite house." It's no surprise, then, that scholars are extremely interested in a structure discovered at Thebes with obvious similarities to that of the "Israelite house."

Could this dwelling have belonged to Hebrew slaves conscripted to work at a nearby Egyptian temple? If so, it is archaeological evidence of an Israelite presence in Egypt. ∎

Left: Ruins of Luxor in ancient Thebes.
Above: Traditional architecture in the desert, Egypt.

17 Why Did God Harden Pharaoh's Heart?

Several times during the account of Moses's confrontation with Pharaoh, the biblical text of Exodus states that "the LORD hardened Pharaoh's heart" (10:20, 27, 11:10). What does this cryptic statement mean? Though Exodus also says in multiple places that Pharaoh hardened his own heart, here it seems the Bible is suggesting that God somehow compelled Pharaoh to do evil.

Insights into Egyptian culture and Hebrew religion can help us understand the meaning of this mysterious expression.

Egyptians saw the heart as the inner spiritual center—or essence—of an individual. They believed that the condition of a person's heart determined a person's eternal destiny. Consequently, after death the heart of the deceased was placed on one side of a scale. On the other side survivors placed a feather, symbolizing truth and justice. This act of weighing the heart represented judgment of the life: If the heart was lighter than the feather, it was believed the deceased would be ushered into an afterlife of happiness. But if the person's heart was heavy—that is, hard—and outweighed the feather, the person was regarded as evil.

The phrase in question may reflect the Hebrew belief that God judges or weighs (Proverbs 21:2)—rather than causes—the hardness of a person's heart. ∎

Above Right: Egyptian pharaoh's statue, the Egyptian Museum, Cairo, Egypt.
Below: *Ramses III*, painted relief, Medinet Habu, Theban Necropolis, Luxor, Egypt.

$\big(18$ The Parting of the Red Sea

Few Bible events capture the imagination like the story of Moses parting the Red Sea. For film buffs and movie connoisseurs, the sight of actor Charlton Heston raising his gnarled staff over the swirling waters in the epic movie *The Ten Commandments* is an iconic moment.

Scholars differ in their interpretations of this event. Did the people of Israel cross a body of water that miraculously parted for them? Or did they only cross a marsh, which happened to ensnare the chariots of the pursuing Egyptians?

One theory connects the events of the Exodus to a massive volcanic eruption that occurred about 1628 BC on the island of Thera (modern-day Santorini) in the Aegean Sea. According to this hypothesis, the volcanic explosion to the north caused a gigantic tidal wave that initially drained the tidal plain over which the Israelites crossed. As the Egyptians followed suit, the water flowed back with devastating force, trapping the charioteers. It's an interesting theory; however, it seems likely that the date of this geological event predates the earliest acceptable date of the Exodus.

Passages in the Bible that say the Israelites crossed the Red Sea "on dry ground" (Exodus 14:22, 29, 15:19) only add to the mystery. ■

Above: *Crossing the Red Sea* by Luca Giordano (1634–1705).

CHAPTER FOUR

Wandering in the Desert

Dahab, Sinai Peninsula, Egypt, mountains in the Sinai desert.

19 Was Mount Sinai in Arabia?

After crossing the Red Sea, according to Exodus, Moses led the people of Israel through the desert to Mount Sinai. There God gave Moses the law (according to Exodus 24:12–18, 34:4–5). But since few of the places mentioned in the biblical text have been positively identified, the precise location of one of the most important events of the Hebrew Bible remains shrouded in mystery.

Mount Sinai has traditionally been identified with a mountain in the Sinai Peninsula, where Saint Catherine's, an Eastern Orthodox monastery, was built in the sixth century AD.

More recently an alternate site has been proposed—to the south in Arabia. Exodus tells us that when Moses fled Egypt, he went into the land of Midian (thought, by some, to be in Arabia). There, God appeared to Moses in the burning bush and said, "When you have brought the people out of Egypt, you shall serve God on this mountain" (Exodus 3:12).

This view is reinforced by a reference to "Mount Sinai in Arabia" in the New Testament (Galatians 4:25). Also, the first-century Jewish historian Josephus mentioned a sacred mountain in Midian that he identified as Sinai.

While the location of Mount Sinai remains unclear, its place in the Bible narrative and Jewish tradition remains unrivaled. ■

Top: Sculpture of Moses by Michelangelo (1475–1564), Church of San Pietro, Rome.
Above: Mount Sinai, Egypt.

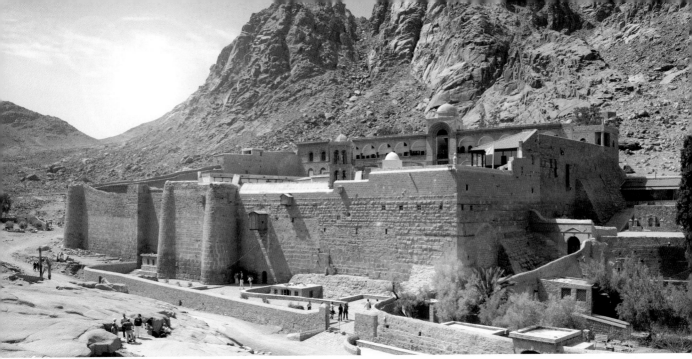

20 Constantin von Tischendorf's Remarkable Discovery

Hoping to discover and decipher the oldest surviving copies of the Bible on earth, Constantin von Tischendorf, an instructor at the University of Leipzig, Germany, traveled first to Italy and then to Egypt.

In 1844 his quest led him to Saint Catherine's Monastery in the Sinai desert. There he noticed 129 pieces of parchment (animal skin), allegedly in a waste bin. To Tischendorf's amazement, the leaves were handwritten pages from a very old Septuagint (a Greek translation of the Hebrew Bible). He requested permission to take them. The monks, upon realizing the value of this third- to fourth-century BC manuscript, only gave him one-third (43) of the leaves.

In 1846 Tischendorf published his find—the books of 1 Chronicles, Nehemiah, Esther, and Jeremiah. In 1853, hoping to retrieve the remaining parchments, Tischendorf returned to the monastery, but this time the monks were not so generous.

For six years Tischendorf could only dream of the monastery's biblical treasures from afar. Then, in 1859, the Russian tsar bankrolled a return trip to the Sinai desert.

It was during this visit to the monastery that Tischendorf was shown a priceless manuscript—the oldest known copy of the entire New Testament and part of the Hebrew Bible, including the Apocrypha. It also contained two other extrabiblical books.

Tischendorf worked for months to transcribe the pages and eventually published them as the *Codex Sinaiticus* (the "Sinai book"). The monastery ended up giving the codex to the Russian tsar in exchange for a surprisingly small amount of money, a silver shrine, and the appointment of their candidate as abbot.

This remarkable story doesn't end there. After the Russian Revolution, Joseph Stalin's government, hungry for cash, sold the 347 leaves of this ancient book to the British Museum for what was then the equivalent of half a million dollars. To this day, tourists to London can see this priceless treasure with their own eyes. ∎

Top: Saint Catherine's Monastery on the Sinai Peninsula, Egypt.   Right: Constantin von Tischendorf.
Below: Page of the *Codex Sinaiticus* with text of Matthew 6:4–32.

21 Manna from Heaven

During their forty-year sojourn in the desert, the Israelites received nourishment from food that miraculously appeared each morning on the ground. "It was like coriander seed, white, and the taste of it was like wafers made with honey" (Exodus 16:31). They called this substance *manna*, which literally means in Hebrew "What is it?"

That's our question too! One theory proposes that manna is a secretion of insects that feed on the sap of tamarisk trees, which are common in the Sinai region. The secretions dry quickly in the hot desert climate, leaving sticky droplets behind.

In 1927, scientists from the Hebrew University in Jerusalem found that these secretions are approximately the size and shape of coriander seeds. And like the biblical manna, the secretions have the taste and texture of honey that has been left to dry.

Then the Lord said to Moses, "Behold, I am about to rain bread from heaven for you, and the people shall go out and gather a day's portion every day, that I may test them, whether they will walk in my law or not." EXODUS 16:4

Local bedouin Arabs still gather these dried secretions early in the morning, just as the Israelites gathered manna. Reportedly, in good years they can gather up to four pounds of the secretions per day, enough to satisfy a grown man. They knead the gathered secretions into a paste to supplement their meager diets.

The bedouin name for this nourishing substance? "Bread from heaven." ∎

Above: *Moses and the Israelites Gathering of Manna* (16th century), Cathedral of Santa Maria Assunta, Padua, Italy.
Left: Coriander seed.

22 Water from the Rock

During their desert wanderings the thirsty Israelites arrived at a place called *Rephidim*. Finding no water, they quarreled with and grumbled at Moses. Many Bible readers have expressed bewilderment at the unusual directions God gave to Moses, as recorded in Exodus 17:6: "Behold, I will stand before you there on the rock at Horeb, and you shall strike the rock, and water shall come out of it, and the people will drink."

Water pouring out of a rock seems impossible to most people. But to bedouins living in the Sinai desert, such an occurrence, though rare, is not perplexing at all. Limestone is porous. Rainwater can collect in the rocks of the Sinai desert. Over time this water becomes trapped in the rock by a buildup of limestone deposits. Striking such a rock can loosen the blockage, which sets the water free.

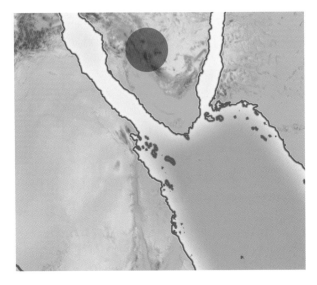

In the 1930s, a British governor of Sinai named Major Claude S. Jarvis and several men were passing through a dry valley when they came across signs of moisture. Thinking the source came from the ground, the men started digging furiously. One of the men accidentally struck the rock wall. In a reprise of Moses at Rephidim, and to the amazement of all, water gushed out of the rock. ∎

All the congregation of the people of Israel moved on from the wilderness of Sin by stages, according to the commandment of the LORD, and camped at Rephidim, but there was no water for the people to drink. Therefore the people quarreled with Moses and said, "Give us water to drink." And Moses said to them, "Why do you quarrel with me? Why do you test the LORD?" . . . And the LORD said to Moses . . . "Behold, I will stand before you there on the rock at Horeb, and you shall strike the rock, and water shall come out of it, and the people will drink." And Moses did so, in the sight of the elders of Israel. And he called the name of the place Massah and Meribah, because of the quarreling of the people of Israel, and because they tested the LORD by saying, "Is the LORD among us or not?"

EXODUS 17:1–2, 5–7

Left: *Moses Strikes the Rock with His Staff* (ca. 1630) by Pieter de Grebber (ca. 1600–1653).

23 Unicorns in the Bible?

People reading the King James Version of the Bible (also known as the Authorized Version) encounter a shock when they get to Numbers 23:22: "God brought them out of Egypt; he hath as it were the strength of an unicorn."

Seriously? The Bible talks about unicorns? Well, the Authorized Version (translated in 1611) does. In fact, it mentions unicorns eight other times (Numbers 24:8; Deuteronomy 33:17; Job 39:9, 10; Psalms 22:21, 29:6, 92:10; and Isaiah 34:7).

Is the Bible saying there really was a horse-like creature with a pointy horn protruding from its forehead? Here are some observations to consider:

- The Hebrew word translated by the KJV as *unicorn* is *re'em*. Almost all other English translations of the Bible render this word as "wild ox."
- In the Talmudic discussions of the Jewish rabbis, we find references to two other similar, mysterious (some would say mythical) creatures—the Keresh (a large deer-like creature with a single black horn) and the Tachash. Some sages claim the Tachash was an enormous kosher animal with a single horn and a hide of six colors. Conjecture is that it only existed in the time of Moses—its beautiful skin was said to have been used in the construction of the tabernacle tent.
- Pliny the Elder, the famous Roman naturalist, mentions the unicorn in his massive *Natural History*. He called it "the fiercest animal, and ... impossible to capture ... alive." He described it as having "the body of a horse, the head of a stag, the feet of an elephant, the tail of a boar, and a single black horn three feet long in the middle of its forehead."
- In early 2016, a British newspaper, *The Guardian*, reported the discovery in Kazakhstan of fragments of *Elasmotherium sibiricum* (the so-called Siberian unicorn). Scientists speculate this massive creature with a single horn probably looked more like a wooly rhinocerous than a horse, and it may have existed alongside humans.[1] ∎

God brought him forth out of Egypt;
he hath as it were the strength of an unicorn:
he shall eat up the nations his enemies,
and shall break their bones,
and pierce them through with his arrows.

NUMBERS 24:8 (KJV)

---

1. Ellen Brait, "Extinct 'Siberian Unicorn' May Have Lived alongside Humans, Fossil Suggests," *The Guardian*, March 29, 2016, accessed May 5, 2017, https://www.theguardian.com/science/2016/mar/29/siberian-unicorn-extinct-humans-fossil-kazakhstan.

Above Right: Unicorn mosaic on a 1213 church floor in Ravenna, Italy.

CHAPTER FIVE

The Conquest of Canaan

Joshua Commanding the Sun to Stand Still upon Gibeon (1816) by John Martin (1789–1854)

24 The Talking Donkey

In the book of Numbers we read that Balak, king of Moab, was concerned about being overrun by the Israelites. They were camped on his border as they prepared to enter the land of Canaan. In his fear, Balak hired a money-hungry prophet named Balaam, from the town of Pethor in upper Mesopotamia, to curse the Israelites using his well-advertised "divination powers." Balak hoped such a magic spell would weaken their military strength.

According to the story in Numbers 22, God sent an angel to thwart Balaam from carrying out this plan. Seeing this angel, Balaam's donkey stopped in its tracks. When Balaam began to beat the animal, it verbally rebuked him! In the end, the shocked Balaam wisely blessed (rather than cursed) the Israelites.

Ancient literature provides several stories or popular fables that feature speaking animals. There were talking cattle in the Egyptian *Tale of Two Brothers* and a conversation between a leopard and gazelle in the Assyrian *Teachings of Ahiqar*.

But a speaking donkey? Talk about a mystery! The author of Numbers doesn't say how this is possible, only that "the LORD opened the mouth of the donkey" (Numbers 22:28). ∎

But God's anger was kindled because he went, and the angel of the LORD took his stand in the way as his adversary. Now he was riding on the donkey, and his two servants were with him. And the donkey saw the angel of the LORD standing in the road, with a drawn sword in his hand. And the donkey turned aside out of the road and went into the field. And Balaam struck the donkey, to turn her into the road. Then the angel of the LORD stood in a narrow path between the vineyards, with a wall on either side. . . . When the donkey saw the angel of the LORD, she lay down under Balaam. And Balaam's anger was kindled, and he struck the donkey with his staff. Then the LORD opened the mouth of the donkey, and she said to Balaam, "What have I done to you, that you have struck me these three times?" And Balaam said to the donkey, "Because you have made a fool of me. I wish I had a sword in my hand, for then I would kill you." And the donkey said to Balaam, "Am I not your donkey, on which you have ridden all your life long to this day? Is it my habit to treat you this way?" And he said, "No."

NUMBERS 22:22–24, 27–30

Above Left: *Balaam and the Angel* (1836) by Gustav Jäger (1808–1871).

25 The Damming of the Jordan River

After their spies returned from Jericho, the Israelites prepared to cross the Jordan River and enter the land of Canaan. However, the river was impassable, because "the Jordan overflows all its banks throughout the time

of harvest" (Joshua 3:15). Meteorologists confirm this fact: snowmelt from Mount Hermon (at the headwaters of the Jordan) annually transforms the river into a wide, swiftly flowing tide that is all but impossible to cross.

The biblical narrative claims, however, that when the feet of the priests carrying the ark of the covenant "dipped in the brink of the water," the Jordan stopped flowing, allowing the Israelites to cross over on dry ground (Joshua 3:15–17).

This biblical account is often assumed by many to be folklore, but interesting historical data lends credence to the story. Over the past two thousand years, the region has experienced at least thirty earthquakes. Ten of these caused great masses of earth from overhanging cliffs to collapse, temporarily damming up the Jordan River and leaving the riverbed downstream dry for up to a day. ■

Top: The Madaba Map, floor mosaic in the early Byzantine Church of Saint George at Madaba, Jordan. It represents the place of John the Baptist's baptism at the mouth of the Jordan River.
Above: *Passage of the Jordan*, biblical engraving.

26 Joshua and the Walls of Jericho

According to the book of Joshua, the Israelites marched around Jericho once a day for six days. On the seventh day, they encircled the city seven times, blew their trumpets and shouted (6:13–16). Jericho's walls collapsed and the Israelites rushed in and conquered the city (6:20).

Over the past century several major archaeological excavations of Jericho have been undertaken, each hoping to uncover some evidence related to this biblical story. The English archaeologist John Garstang worked at the site from 1930 to 1936 and astonished the scholarly world by announcing that the walls of Jericho had indeed fallen sometime before 1400 BC, which fits with the biblical chronology.

Two decades later, his findings were challenged by another English archaeologist, Dame Kathleen Kenyon, who concluded that Jericho was destroyed over a century before the generally accepted date for the Israelites' arrival into Canaan. Based on Kenyon's data, the walls were destroyed long before Joshua's time and there was no city for the Israelites to conquer.

After a reexamination of the data in 1990, however, Kenyon's findings were called into question. A piece of charcoal from Jericho's debris layer was carbon-dated to 1410 BC—a date that fits with the biblical chronology. Pottery fragments and other artifacts are also consistent with the claim that the walls of Jericho somehow collapsed in Joshua's day. ■

Top: Ruins of ancient Jericho.
Above: *The Battle of Jericho* (1603), fresco by Tarquinio Ligustri (b. 1564), Basilica di San Vitale, Rome, Italy.

27 Nonprofit Battles

In the ancient world, nations typically went to war to increase their wealth, power, and size. Kings eyed greedily the territory and possessions of their weaker neighbors. What's more, they wanted more subjects they could coerce into paying heavy taxes or force into slave labor.

Yet when the Israelites conquered Jericho, they acquired nothing! Joshua 6:17–19 says the Israelites were forbidden to take the city's inhabitants as slaves. They also weren't allowed to seize Jericho's livestock or wealth. Not only was everything destroyed, but Joshua decreed that the site must forever lie in ruin (Joshua 6:26). When one Israelite man violated this ban, he was put to death (Joshua 7:24–26). This was not the typical outcome of an ancient battle.

According to the Bible, God commanded the Israelites to go to war against the Canaanites not only to claim the land, but also as a judgment for their idolatry and wicked behavior (Deut. 9:5; Lev. 18:24-25). In the case of Jericho, and sometimes in later instances, to emphasize that they were God's weapons of judgment, the Israelites were not allowed to profit from their battle. In the Bible, the battle of Jericho is not about profit but about punishing the wicked. ■

Left: *Gates of Paradise,* depicting the fall of Jericho, by Lorenzo Ghiberti (1378–1455), Baptistry of Saint John, Florence, Italy.
Right: Ruins of Tell es-Sultan Neolithic tower.

28 The Merneptah Inscription

There are few references to ancient Israel outside the Bible. One that has been of considerable interest to scholars is an inscription found in an Egyptian temple at the end of the last century. It sheds light on important questions from Israel's early history: the date of the Exodus and the Israelites' conquest of Canaan.

In 1896, the renowned Egyptologist Flinders Petrie was excavating in the mortuary temple of Pharaoh Merneptah in Thebes when he discovered what has come to be known as the Merneptah Stele (or the Israel Stela). A stele (or stela) is a cut, standing stone with writing on it. Steles were used in ancient times to chronicle important events in the reign of a ruler. As it turns out, the Merneptah Stele preserves what is the most important mention of Israel outside the Bible—and the only mention of Israel in Egyptian records.

While describing a military victory by Pharaoh Merneptah over Libya and its allies around 1200 BC, the stele also says, "Israel is laid waste, its seed is not." The majority of biblical scholars see this as a reference to Egypt's conquest of a people group in Canaan at that time.

With the discovery of this stele, historians are able to confirm that if the Exodus happened, it must have taken place sometime before the reign of Merneptah (1213–1203 BC), since the Israelites were by then living in Canaan and were known to ancient Egyptians. They were also numerous enough for the Egyptian king to mention them by name as a group of people he fought.

The Merneptah Stele represents the first documented instance of the name *Israel* in the historical record. It indicates that the Israelites must have been in Canaan before Israel was "laid waste" by Merneptah and his victory stele raised. ■

Above: Replica of ancient Egyptian stele called the Israeli Stele.
Left: Merneptah Stele on the west bank of the Nile.

CHAPTER SIX

The Historical Books

Ancient goat skin Torah scroll.

29 The Revenge of Samson

The mighty Samson was one of Israel's judges (military deliverers). He was betrayed by the beautiful Delilah. When Philistines captured him, they shaved his head, gouged out his eyes, and forced him to grind grain like an ox.

According to the biblical text, Samson was brought out to entertain the assembled Philistines. He asked to stand between two pillars in the center of the building so he could lean against them: "And Samson said, 'Let me die with the Philistines.' Then he bowed with all his strength, and the house fell upon the lords and upon all the people who were in it. So the dead whom he killed at his death were more than those whom he had killed during his life" (Judges 16:30).

It would, of course, require unearthly strength to accomplish such a feat. The book of Judges connects Samson's long hair (part of his vow as a Nazarite) to his superhuman might. According to Judges 16:19, when the Philistines cut off Samson's hair, "his strength left him." However, the Philistines allowed his hair to grow back while in prison (Judges 16:22), and his strength returned.

Leaving such "hairy" mysteries aside, archaeology provides us with this fascinating information: excavations in Israel show that the roofs of Philistine temples were indeed supported by twin central pillars, spaced between six and seven feet apart, making it theoretically possible for them to be pushed simultaneously by a large, strong man. ■

30 Boaz's New Wife, Field, and Shoe

The book of Ruth mentions several odd and ancient practices that cause modern-day Bible readers to scratch their heads.

Ruth was a young, widowed Moabite woman who relocated to Israel with her elderly, widowed mother-in-law, Naomi. At Naomi's instructions, Ruth helped herself to unharvested grain along the edges of some neighbors' wheat fields. This wasn't stealing; this was in accord with a Hebrew law designed to insure that the poor in Israel could always find food (Leviticus 19:9–10).

When Ruth stumbled into the fields of Boaz, Naomi's relative, Naomi decided to play matchmaker. She reminded Boaz of a Hebrew law that called a close relative to purchase ("redeem") the property of a deceased relative in order to keep his land in the family (Leviticus 25:25–28). This custom also involved marrying the man's widow and having children with her so as to perpetuate the family line.

Boaz admitted that he was not Naomi's closest living male relative. But when the man who was more eligible declined the opportunity to redeem the land and marry Ruth (4:1–4), Boaz agreed to take her as his wife.

The men sealed the arrangement in an odd way. The man who waived his right to purchase the land and marry Ruth took off his sandal and gave it to Boaz (Ruth 4:7–8). This was a way of saying, "Boaz, you—not I—now have the legal right to walk on the land in question. It belongs to you."

Now you know how and why in one day Boaz gained a wife, some real estate, and a single sandal! ■

Left: *The Death of Samson* by Gustave Doré (1832–1883).
Top Right: *Ruth in Boaz's Field* (1828)
by Julius Schnorr von Carolsfeld (1794–1872).

31 Esther: Prejudice and Genocide

During the reign of Persian king Xerxes I (Ahasuerus), Queen Esther and her cousin Mordecai worked together to save the Hebrew people, the Jews, from a genocidal plot. According to the Bible, in the book of Esther, it happened like this: Haman, a high official in the royal city of Susa, became enraged when Mordecai refused to bow down to him. Learning of Mordecai's Jewish ancestry, Haman convinced the king to issue a proclamation calling for the extermination of all the Jews in Persia.

However, Esther prevailed upon the king to rescind the proclamation, and Haman's evil plot was exposed. In a final irony, Haman met his end on the very gallows he had constructed for Mordecai.

The story of Esther is so captivating that some have considered it little more than a Jewish folktale. However, numerous details of the story reflect an intimate familiarity with Persian life and culture in the fifth century BC.

First, the book records the first Feast of Purim, a day of grateful celebration for the Jews' deliverance through the courage of Mordecai and Esther.

Second, the book ends with Mordecai rising to a position second only to the king. There is an intriguing mention in the historical sources of someone with a similar name, Marduka, identified as a scribe at Susa. ∎

_____

"For if you keep silent at this time, relief and deliverance will rise for the Jews from another place, but you and your father's house will perish. And who knows whether you have not come to the kingdom for such a time as this?" ESTHER 4:14

_____

Top Right: *Queen Esther* (1878) by Edwin Long (1829–1891).
Above: Gate of All Nations or Gate of Xerxes in the ruins of ancient Persepolis, capital of Achaemenid Empire in Shiraz, Iran.

32 The Mysterious Urim and Thummim

Early in his reign Saul had successfully used something called the Urim and Thummim to discover which of his soldiers had violated his orders in a battle with the Philistines. Now, as his troubled rule neared its end, he prepared to fight the Philistines. Stricken with fear, Saul sought supernatural guidance. But since, according to the biblical account, God had rejected the disobedient Saul as king over Israel (1 Samuel 15:10–11, 23, 26), "when Saul inquired of the Lord, the Lord did not answer him, either by dreams, or by Urim, or by prophets" (1 Samuel 28:6).

What was this Urim and Thummim? How were they used in ancient Israel to discern God's will? Little is known about their appearance or size or how exactly they provided guidance. They are mentioned in the book of Exodus as being kept by the high priest in a "breastpiece of judgment" (28:30). Biblical references suggest they may have been a pair of objects drawn or shaken from a bag, with one object signifying a positive answer and the other a negative response.

Now Samuel had died, and all Israel had mourned for him and buried him in Ramah, his own city. And Saul had put the mediums and the necromancers out of the land. The Philistines assembled and came and encamped at Shunem. And Saul gathered all Israel, and they encamped at Gilboa. When Saul saw the army of the Philistines, he was afraid, and his heart trembled greatly. And when Saul inquired of the Lord, the Lord did not answer him, either by dreams, or by Urim, or by prophets.

1 SAMUEL 28:3–6

To the Western mind, the use of such means appears to signify reliance upon blind chance—like flipping a coin. The Israelites, however, believed that God worked through the Urim and Thummim to reveal his will. The priests used these sacred objects to avoid making decisions based on flawed human reasoning. (See also Proverbs 16:33.)

Some Bible scholars believe the Urim and Thummim were probably lost when Nebuchadnezzar destroyed the temple. There is no historical suggestion that the Israelites used them after their return from captivity. ■

Above: *Saul and David* (1658) by Rembrandt (1606–1669).

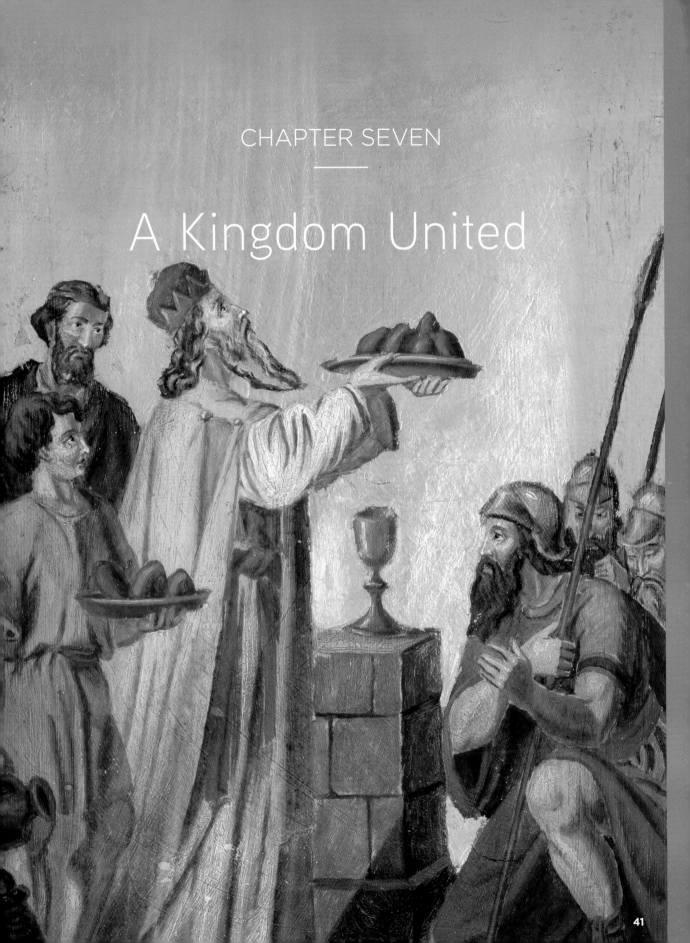

CHAPTER SEVEN

A Kingdom United

33 Miracles vs. Magic: A Witch at En-dor

Having been rebuffed by God as king over Israel, King Saul was determined to obtain supernatural knowledge about what would happen in his impending battle with the Philistines. Saul disguised himself and traveled to the village of En-dor to visit a spiritual medium known to reside there.

Meeting with this witch required Saul to make a dangerous journey around enemy forces. And consulting a medium reversed a policy that Saul had established early in his reign, when he "expelled the mediums and spiritists from the land" (1 Samuel 28:3, NIV).

So Saul disguised himself and put on other garments and went, he and two men with him. And they came to the woman by night. And he said, "Divine for me by a spirit and bring up for me whomever I shall name to you." The woman said to him, "Surely you know what Saul has done, how he has cut off the mediums and the necromancers from the land. Why then are you laying a trap for my life to bring about my death?" But Saul swore to her by the LORD, "As the LORD lives, no punishment shall come upon you for this thing." Then the woman said, "Whom shall I bring up for you?" He said, "Bring up Samuel for me." When the woman saw Samuel, she cried out with a loud voice. And the woman said to Saul, "Why have you deceived me? You are Saul."

1 SAMUEL 28:8–12

At Saul's request, the medium agreed to conjure up the ghost of Samuel—and then was terrified when the dead prophet actually appeared! This reaction may suggest the medium was a fraud (who really didn't expect anything to happen). Or she may have been frightened because of the prophet Samuel's well-known opposition to the practice of witchcraft (1 Samuel 15:23).

At any rate, the news could not have been worse. Samuel told Saul that Israel would be defeated and that he and his sons would die on the battlefield. At these words, and because "he had eaten nothing all day and all night" (1 Samuel 28:20), Saul became a shivering wreck.

In a final irony, the medium insisted on preparing Saul a meal. After the devastated king ate, he "rose and went away that night" (1 Samuel 28:25). This would be his last meal. ■

Left: Traditional site of the biblical En-dor, Israel.
Right: *The Ghost of Samuel Appearing to Saul* (1800) by William Blake (1757–1827).

34 An Unlikely King

Since the beginning of time, people have valued external appearance. It's no surprise, then, that Israel's first king, Saul, is described in 1 Samuel 9:2 as "a handsome young man. . . . From his shoulders upward he was taller than any of the people." Saul's internal condition, however, proved not to be so attractive. He was impulsive, and, over time, he became consumed by jealousy, rage, and paranoia (1 Samuel 18:8–11).

After Saul was later disqualified as Israel's king (1 Samuel 15:26), God sent the prophet Samuel to the Bethlehem home of a man named Jesse to anoint a new king. When Samuel arrived, he scanned Jesse's sons to see which one most looked the part. His gaze fixed on Eliab—a strapping, good-looking young man.

According to 1 Samuel 16, while the prophet gawked at Eliab—the obvious candidate in Samuel's estimation—God told him, "Do not look on his appearance or on the height of his stature, because I have rejected him. For the Lord sees not as man sees: man looks on the outward appearance, but the Lord looks on the heart" (verse 7).

Samuel was then prompted to select the youngest son, David, and anoint him as Israel's next king. The Bible indicates that God saw something very significant in David's character. He was "a man after his own heart" (1 Samuel 13:14).

The anointing of David, Israel's most beloved king, shows how the God of the Bible challenges human expectations. ■

Left: *Samuel Anoints David* (3rd century AD), Dura Europos, Syria.
Right: Detail from the replica statue of David in Piazza della Signoria, Florence. A masterpiece of Renaissance sculpture, created by Michelangelo in 1504.

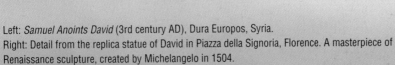

35 The Daring Capture of Jerusalem

When David and his men prepared to capture Jerusalem and make it their new capital, the Jebusite inhabitants were so confident of the city's defenses that they taunted the Israelites: "You will not come in here, but the blind and the lame will ward you off" (2 Samuel 5:6).

Indeed, the walled Jebusite city (then called Jebus) was surrounded by steep hillsides and appeared impregnable. David, however, had learned about a hidden Achilles heel in the city's defenses: a carefully concealed tunnel that brought water into the city from a spring outside the walls. David instructed his men: "Whoever would strike the Jebusites, let him get up the water shaft to attack 'the lame and blind,' who are hated by David's soul" (2 Samuel 5:8).

Until recent times Bible scholars had little idea where this "water shaft" was. In the mid-nineteenth century one of the earliest English archaeologists of the Jerusalem area, General Sir Charles Warren, discovered a vertical shaft that led from the Gihon Spring (Jerusalem's only natural water source) to within the walls of the ancient city. To determine whether it would have been feasible to enter the city through the tunnel, a group of archaeologists attempted to climb up the narrow forty-five-foot shaft. Without using special climbing equipment, they were able to scale what has come to be known as Warren's Shaft. Some archaeologists dispute that this shaft is linked to David's conquest; others believe it was through this tunnel that David's soldiers gained access to Jerusalem three thousand years ago. ■

36 The Tel Dan Inscription

For a long time many historians put King David in the same category as King Arthur. In other words, they regarded him as a mythical figure, the stuff of legends.

Why would scholars conclude such a thing about a man mentioned in the Hebrew Bible more times than anyone else except the great Moses? One simple reason: researchers could find no evidence outside the Bible for either David's life or his kingship.

Or, they concluded, if the biblical David did exist, he must have been nothing more than a local chieftain. He could not have been the leader of a large nation; otherwise there would be extrabiblical evidence of his reign.

This all changed in 1993. Archaeologist Avraham Biran, while digging at Tel Dan in northern Israel, found a stone slab (stele) that featured an Aramean inscription. This bit of ancient writing caused a giant stir in academic and biblical circles because it made reference to "the House of David." Not only was

this common terminology among ancient peoples—describing the king of a nation as a father over a house—it is also the same language used in 2 Samuel 3:6.

This marker, erected by one of Israel's fiercest enemies and dated to 841 BC (only a century or so after David's death), is seen as strong evidence of a real-life King David and a royal dynasty.

You can see the Tel Dan Stele for yourself. It's on display at the Israel Museum. ■

Above: The Tel Dan Stele on display at the Israel Museum, Jerusalem, courtesy of Oren Rozen.

37 The Queen of the South

We read in 2 Chronicles that King Solomon had an illustrious visitor: "Now when the queen of Sheba heard of the fame of Solomon, she came to Jerusalem to test him with hard questions, having a very great retinue and camels bearing spices and very much gold and precious stones. And when she came to Solomon, she told him all that was on her mind" (2 Chronicles 9:1).

Some scholars think the biblical queen of Sheba hailed from south Arabia in what today would be Yemen. This is close to the Red Sea, on major trade routes, and convenient to shipping lanes with Africa and India. In 1 Kings 10:10 we learn that the queen's gift of gold amounted to 120 "talents"—or an astounding 9,000 pounds. Clearly she ruled over a kingdom of fabulous wealth. Arabian spices—including cinnamon, cardamom, nutmeg, ginger, and cloves—were highly valued throughout the Middle East and beyond.

While the journey was some 1,400 miles and would have taken many weeks, the time spent with Solomon greatly enlightened this mysterious queen. And she must have left a lasting impression on Solomon and the people of Israel. Curiously, Jesus is recorded to have mentioned her to teachers of religious law: "The queen of the South will rise up at the judgment with this generation and condemn it, for she came from the ends of the earth to hear the wisdom of Solomon, and behold, something greater than Solomon is here" (Matthew 12:42). ■

Top: Sabaean Wall on Diga Ruins at Marib, Yemen.
Right: *Solomon and the Queen of Sheba* by Giovanni Demin (1789–1859).

38 Solomon's Temple

King Solomon's beautifully crafted temple took seven years to build. It housed the ark of the covenant, along with many other gold and silver vessels (1 Kings 6). Once it was finished, Solomon and the people offered sacrifices to God at the temple's dedication. When they did, the biblical record says, "fire came down from heaven and consumed the burnt offering and the sacrifices, and the glory of the LORD filled the temple" (2 Chronicles 7:1). In the Hebrew Bible, fire or a cloud often symbolizes God's presence with his people.

This First Temple was destroyed by Babylonian king Nebuchadnezzar in 587 BC, as described in 2 Kings 25. The Babylonians likely took any remaining gold and silver articles from the temple, but some people believe these valuable treasures are still hidden at or near the temple site.

It's worth noting that archaeologists have made a few interesting discoveries at the foot of the Temple Mount, in the area called Ophel between the temple and the royal palace. Among the findings are a portion of city wall and a gatehouse, which some associate with Solomon's First Temple (1 Kings 5 and 7). While no obvious temple artifacts have been found to date, these remains suggest a structure existed in that location from the beginning of the ninth century BC. This is a possible date for the reign of King Solomon.

The mysteries surrounding the First Temple continue to fascinate modern researchers. Many remain hopeful of finding clear evidence from the First Temple. However, due to the sensitive nature of excavating in and around Jerusalem, where the sacred claims of many cultures and religions clash, archaeologists aren't holding their breath. ◾

Above: The Dome of the Rock stands at the traditional location of Solomon's temple.

CHAPTER EIGHT

Prophets and Seers

The Prophet Elijah Receiving Bread and Water from an Angel, artist unknown, Santa Maria della Salute, Venice, Italy.

39 The Battle of the Gods

King Ahab of Israel married the Phoenician princess Jezebel.

Jezebel's name literally means "Baal is the Prince." The book of 1 Kings describes her as a devoted worshiper of the Canaanite gods Baal and Asherah. Baal was believed by many to be the god of storms and fertility. This god is often pictured grasping a lightning bolt amid storm clouds.

Using her royal influence, Jezebel set about making Baal worship the major religion of the entire northern kingdom. She even called for the execution of prophets who served the God of Abraham, Isaac, and Jacob (see 1 Kings 16:29–34, 18:3–4, 13).

Against this backdrop, the writer of 1 Kings prepares us for an epic battle of the gods atop Mount Carmel.

There the prophet Elijah issued a challenge to 450 prophets of Baal and 400 other pagan prophets (1 Kings 18:19). He called on them to convince Baal to demonstrate power by casting down lightning bolts and consuming their sacrifice. They prayed fervently and nothing happened (1 Kings 18:26).

Elijah then constructed an altar, dug a trench around it, drenched the offering with water, and called on the God of Israel. Immediately "the fire of the LORD fell, and consumed the burnt sacrifice, and the wood, and the stones, and the dust, and licked up the water that was in the trench" (1 Kings 18:38, KJV).

After this dramatic display, Elijah prompted the spectators to seize the prophets of Baal and kill them (1 Kings 18:39–40). ∎

40 Ezekiel's Vision of Dry Bones

Through the prophet Ezekiel, the Jewish people living in exile received this wonderful promise from God: "I will take you from the nations and gather you from all the countries and bring you into your own land" (Ezekiel 36:24).

Yet it was the wild vision accompanying this promise that was most encouraging. Ezekiel saw a valley filled with dry bones. Then he watched as the bones gradually came back to life! No wonder the prophet exclaimed: "They will say, 'This land that was desolate has become like the garden of Eden, and the waste and desolate and ruined cities are now fortified and inhabited'" (Ezekiel 36:35).

The Israelites' hope sprang from the familiarity of this imagery. After most Mesopotamian and Egyptian wars, it was not uncommon for corpses to go unburied. Assyrian records describe the destruction of their enemies in these terms. The prophet's vision of dry bones being reassembled, re-covered with flesh, and reanimated surely inspired and encouraged the exiled Jews.

For centuries, the land of ancient Israel remained a sparsely populated and barren land under the control of various nations. Then in 1948, Israel became a sovereign, thriving nation. Many students of biblical prophecy see the flourishing modern-day Jewish state as fulfillment of Ezekiel's ancient prophecy. ∎

Above: The excavations at Samaria.
Ruins of Ahab's Palace.

41 Hezekiah's Tunnel

Before the reign of King David, Jerusalem was surrounded by valleys and strong defensive fortifications. Yet in a region with scarce rainfall, the city had one major vulnerability: its only water source, the Gihon Spring, lay outside the city walls. Efforts to disguise this spring were detected by David's men, who exploited this chink in Jerusalem's armor. That's how the Israelites were originally able to capture the city (1 Chronicles 11:5).

Three centuries later, Assyria was threatening Jerusalem. In ancient times, walled cities were typically surrounded until their inhabitants ran out of food and water

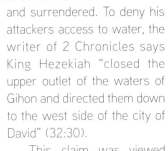

and surrendered. To deny his attackers access to water, the writer of 2 Chronicles says King Hezekiah "closed the upper outlet of the waters of Gihon and directed them down to the west side of the city of David" (32:30).

This claim was viewed with suspicion until the 1838 discovery of Hezekiah's Tunnel, dated to the late eighth century BC. This ancient engineering project enabled the water of the Gihon Spring to flow through a nearly 1,500-foot tunnel to a protected location on the far (western) side of the city.

Jerusalem received its needed water supply as well as (according to the biblical accounts) military deliverance when "the angel of the LORD" killed 185,000 Assyrian soldiers, ending the siege (see 2 Kings 19:35). Centuries later, as the story is told in John 9:1–7, another miracle occurred at the pool of Siloam, the endpoint of Hezekiah's Tunnel. ◾

42 Jonah and the Great Fish

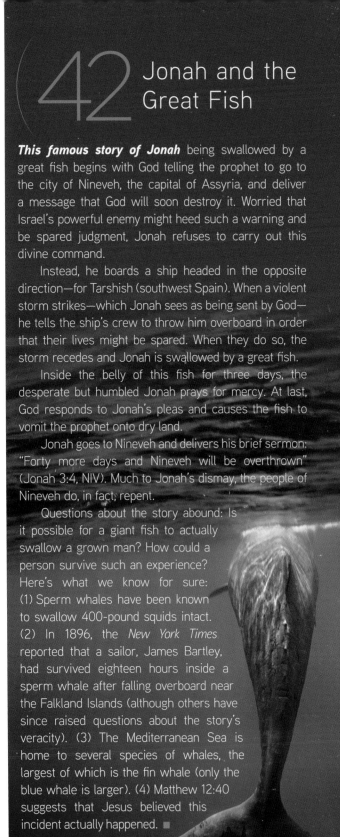

This famous story of Jonah being swallowed by a great fish begins with God telling the prophet to go to the city of Nineveh, the capital of Assyria, and deliver a message that God will soon destroy it. Worried that Israel's powerful enemy might heed such a warning and be spared judgment, Jonah refuses to carry out this divine command.

Instead, he boards a ship headed in the opposite direction—for Tarshish (southwest Spain). When a violent storm strikes—which Jonah sees as being sent by God—he tells the ship's crew to throw him overboard in order that their lives might be spared. When they do so, the storm recedes and Jonah is swallowed by a great fish.

Inside the belly of this fish for three days, the desperate but humbled Jonah prays for mercy. At last, God responds to Jonah's pleas and causes the fish to vomit the prophet onto dry land.

Jonah goes to Nineveh and delivers his brief sermon: "Forty more days and Nineveh will be overthrown" (Jonah 3:4, NIV). Much to Jonah's dismay, the people of Nineveh do, in fact, repent.

Questions about the story abound: Is it possible for a giant fish to actually swallow a grown man? How could a person survive such an experience? Here's what we know for sure: (1) Sperm whales have been known to swallow 400-pound squids intact. (2) In 1896, the *New York Times* reported that a sailor, James Bartley, had survived eighteen hours inside a sperm whale after falling overboard near the Falkland Islands (although others have since raised questions about the story's veracity). (3) The Mediterranean Sea is home to several species of whales, the largest of which is the fin whale (only the blue whale is larger). (4) Matthew 12:40 suggests that Jesus believed this incident actually happened. ◾

Left: Hezekiah's Tunnel, photo courtesy of Tamar Hayardeni.
Right: Sperm whale.

43 The Moabite Stone's Version of History

"I am Mesha, son of Chemosh-gad, king of Moab"—
so begins a remarkable inscription on a stele (stone monument) discovered in Jordan known as the Moabite Stone, which sheds light on the stark contrast between the religion of Israel and that of its neighbors.

King Mesha lived in the ninth century BC and is mentioned only once in the Bible: "Now Mesha king of Moab raised sheep, and he had to pay the king of Israel a tribute … But after Ahab died, the king of Moab rebelled against the king of Israel" (2 Kings 3:4–5, NIV).

The Moabite Stone inscription presents King Mesha's account of the ensuing battle after his rebellion against Israel.

The inscription includes the earliest mention of the God of Israel outside the Bible, and it paints a revealing picture of the difference between the Israelite religion and that of the Moabites, who worshiped the god Chemosh. According to the book of 2 Kings, the Israelite leaders sought guidance from God, but the king of Moab "took his firstborn son . . . and offered him as a sacrifice on the city wall" in an attempt to appease Chemosh and drive the Israelites from his land (3:27, NIV). ■

In the eighteenth year of Jehoshaphat king of Judah, Jehoram the son of Ahab became king over Israel in Samaria, and he reigned twelve years. He did what was evil in the sight of the Lᴏʀᴅ, though not like his father and mother, for he put away the pillar of Baal that his father had made. Nevertheless, he clung to the sin of Jeroboam the son of Nebat, which he made Israel to sin; he did not depart from it.

Now Mesha king of Moab was a sheep breeder, and he had to deliver to the king of Israel 100,000 lambs and the wool of 100,000 rams. But when Ahab died, the king of Moab rebelled against the king of Israel.

2 KINGS 3:1–5

Right: Mesha Stele, Louvre Museum.

44 Elijah's Chariot of Fire

The Bible doesn't explain why fire is a recurring theme in the exploits of the Israelite prophet Elijah. Perhaps it's because of his fiery nature: zealous, intense, intolerant of pagan religion and idolatry.

Consider: In response to Elijah's prayer on Mount Carmel, a flash of lightning comes down from heaven, igniting a sacrificial offering (1 Kings 18:38). When King Ahaziah twice sends messengers to the prophet demanding that he appear before the king, the messengers are consumed each time by divine fire (2 Kings 1:10–12). Then there's the mysterious event from the end of Elijah's story.

As he and his successor, Elisha, were walking along, "there appeared a chariot of fire and horses of fire which separated the two of them. And Elijah went up by a whirlwind to heaven. Elisha saw it and cried out, 'My father, my father, the chariots of Israel and its horsemen!'" (2 Kings 2:11–12, NASB).

With Elijah gone, Elisha takes up his mantle and assumes the prophetic task. Interestingly, the Bible tells us Elisha proceeds to carry out his prophetic mission via miracles involving water, not fire. ■

Above: Scene of Elijah ascending to heaven and Elisha with Elijah's mantle (17th century), artist unknown, Basilica del Carmine, Padova, Italy.

45 Elisha and the Two Bears

Bible readers often puzzle over a bizarre incident from the ministry of Elisha the prophet:

> He went up from there to Bethel, and while he was going up on the way, some small boys came out of the city and jeered at him, saying, "Go up, you baldhead! Go up, you baldhead!" And he turned around, and when he saw them, he cursed them in the name of the LORD. And two she-bears came out of the woods and tore forty-two of the boys. From there he went on to Mount Carmel, and from there he returned to Samaria. (2 Kings 2:23–25)

Besides demonstrating that Elisha probably wouldn't have made a great middle school or high school teacher, this scene raises a lot of questions: Was Elisha just having a bad day? Was he *that* sensitive about his hair loss? Couldn't he take a little kidding? Isn't this a rather extreme reaction?

Here is what we can say about this strange story. First, there were bears in ancient Israel—specifically the Syrian brown bear. Second, many Hebrew scholars note that the Hebrew word translated "small boys" here can also be translated "young men." Third, because there were at least forty-two males taunting Elisha—in other words, a mini-mob—perhaps his life was in danger; therefore, his reaction was probably one of self-defense. Fourth, their catcalls to "Go up, you baldhead!" may have been a derisive reference to the claim that Elisha's prophetic mentor, Elijah, had been taken up to heaven in a whirlwind. Since a bald scalp was viewed as a curse (Isaiah 3:24), this gang of youths was likely demonstrating immense disrespect for a spokesperson of God. ■

Left: Illustration of boys being mauled by bears for mocking Elisha.

46 Asher Shall Dip His Foot in Oil

A little-known prophecy about Asher, the grandson of Noah, has led to speculation regarding the potential for great oil wealth in Israel: "Most blessed of sons be Asher; let him be the favorite of his brothers, and let him dip his foot in oil" (Deuteronomy 33:24).

The ancient world would never have interpreted this statement as referring to petroleum. "Oil" in the Bible refers to olive oil, a food staple. Properly understood within the historical context, the prophecy most likely refers to Asher's family being blessed, illustrated by an abundance of the vital commodity of olive oil.

Nevertheless, in the last fifty years, this reference to "oil" caught the eye of some who believed the text might provide a clue to the location of vast petroleum deposits. An examination of maps of Israel pinpointed the "toe" of Asher's territory at the Roman port of Caesarea on the shores of the Mediterranean Sea.

An extensive drilling program commenced in 1982, but after two years it ended without producing a single barrel of oil. Decades of exploratory drilling throughout the country have yielded meager results. In recent years, however, massive oil and gas reserves have been discovered in the Mediterranean Sea off Israel's coast—leading some people to wonder if these discoveries might be a fulfillment of the prophecy of blessing upon the descendants of Asher. ∎

And of Asher he said,
"Most blessed of sons be Asher;
    let him be the favorite of his brothers,
    and let him dip his foot in oil.
Your bars shall be iron and bronze,
    and as your days, so shall your strength be.
"There is none like God, O Jeshurun,
    who rides through the heavens to your help,
    through the skies in his majesty.
The eternal God is your dwelling place,
    and underneath are the everlasting arms.
And he thrust out the enemy before you
    and said, 'Destroy.'
So Israel lived in safety,
    Jacob lived alone,
in a land of grain and wine,
    whose heavens drop down dew.
Happy are you, O Israel! Who is like you,
    a people saved by the LORD,
the shield of your help,
    and the sword of your triumph!
Your enemies shall come fawning to you,
    and you shall tread upon their backs."

DEUTERONOMY 33:24–29

Mediterranean Sea and Israeli coast.

(47

The Missing Books

Some readers have questions about all those books referred to *in* the Bible that are not actually books *of* the Bible.

These twenty or so documents are not part of the biblical canon (writings widely regarded as "sacred"). It is commonly speculated that these books originated as oral traditions and were eventually written on scrolls.

Some of these noncanonical books were composed by biblical figures. The author of 1 Chronicles references books by Nathan and Gad, who were prophets during the reign of David: "As for the events of King David's reign, from beginning to end, they are written in . . . the records of Nathan the prophet and the records of Gad the seer" (29:29, NIV).

A writer named Jashar recorded a miraculous event in Israel's history: "So the sun stood still, and the moon stopped, till the nation avenged itself on its enemies, as it is written in the Book of Jashar" (Joshua 10:13, NIV). This "Book of Jashar" is also quoted in 2 Samuel 1:18–27. The book of Numbers quotes an extrabiblical text when describing the borders of Israel: "The Arnon is the border of Moab, between Moab and the Amorites. That is why the Book of the Wars of the LORD says . . ." (21:13–15, NIV).

While these books mentioned in the Bible are long lost, scholars suspect they originally served as valuable, credible historical sources for those writing the books of the Bible. ∎

[David] ordered that the people of Judah be taught this lament of the bow (it is written in the Book of Jashar):

"A gazelle lies slain on your heights, Israel.
*   How the mighty have fallen!*

"Tell it not in Gath,
*   proclaim it not in the streets of Ashkelon,*
lest the daughters of the Philistines be glad,
*   lest the daughters of the uncircumcised rejoice.*

"Mountains of Gilboa,
*   may you have neither dew nor rain,*
*   may no showers fall on your terraced fields.*
For there the shield of the mighty was despised,
*   the shield of Saul—no longer rubbed with oil."*

2 SAMUEL 1:18–21 (NIV)

Above: Hebrew handwritten Torah.

CHAPTER NINE

Judah and Israel: The Kingdom Is Divided

Antique map of Israel (1836).

48

Hooks in Their Jaws

What does the biblical text mean when it speaks of someone putting a hook into the jaw of another?

For example, in a diatribe against a mysterious enemy of Israel, the prophet Ezekiel ascribes these words to God: "Thus says the Lord GOD: Behold, I am against you, O Gog, chief prince of Meshech and Tubal. And I will turn you about and put hooks into your jaws, and I will bring you out, and all your army, horses and horsemen, all of them clothed in full armor, a great host, all of them with buckler and shield, wielding swords" (38:3–4).

Historians help us understand this mysterious threat. They tell us that the Assyrians often put actual, metal hooks into the jaws of their defeated enemies. They did this for psychological reasons—to inflict pain and humiliation. They did this practically to control and/or deport prisoners of war to other lands and kingdoms as trade. Many Assyrian wall reliefs and some of their written history reflect this painful practice.

In one such depiction, Assyrian king Esarhaddon (680–669 BC) is depicted on a stele (stone monument) found at Zinjirli in Syria as leading Baal of Tyre and Tirhakah of Egypt by a rope tied through a ring secured in their lips. Another shows the king of Ishmael with pierced cheeks and a large ring in his jaw.

Most scholars, therefore, believe that the prophet Ezekiel was painting an encouraging picture for Israel—that their brutal enemies would ultimately be defeated. ■

49

The Writing on the Wall

Daniel 5:1 describes King Belshazzar at ease in Babylon, presiding over "a great feast for a thousand of his lords." The city was reported to have boasted some of the most impressive structures of Mesopotamia, including the famous Hanging Gardens and the Ishtar Gate. Unaware of any looming threat, the assembled guests are described as praising "the gods of gold and silver, bronze, iron, wood, and stone" (5:4).

But then we read that "immediately the fingers of a human hand appeared and wrote on the plaster of the wall" (Daniel 5:5). At this, Belshazzar turned pale and his knees buckled. Upon the advice of his queen, he called in Daniel to interpret the writing. Daniel studied the inscription and announced its somber meaning: "God has numbered the days of your kingdom and brought it to an end" (5:26).

Then they brought in the golden vessels that had been taken out of the temple, the house of God in Jerusalem, and the king and his lords, his wives, and his concubines drank from them. . . .

Immediately the fingers of a human hand appeared and wrote on the plaster of the wall of the king's palace, opposite the lampstand. And the king saw the hand as it wrote. Then the king's color changed, and his thoughts alarmed him; his limbs gave way, and his knees knocked together.

DANIEL 5:3, 5–6

How could this be? Ringed by three massive defensive walls, Babylon was considered impregnable. Yet, as predicted in the Bible by Daniel and also confirmed by extrabiblical sources, Belshazzar's Persian enemy devised an ingenious plan to circumvent the city's immense fortifications: They diverted the course of the Euphrates River, which ran through the city. When the water quit flowing, Persian soldiers slipped into the city via the dried-up riverbed.

In 539 BC the great city of Babylon fell to the Persian army in one night! ■

Left: Black basalt monument of King Esarhaddon.
Photo courtesy of Osama Shukir Muhammed Amin FRCP (Glasg).

Above: *Daniel Interpreting the Writing on the Wall* by Gustave Doré (1832–1883).
Right: *Prophet Daniel* (1904–1906) by Leopold Bruckner (n.d.), Saint Nicholas Church, Brussels.

50 What Destroyed Sennacherib's Army?

In 701 BC, Jerusalem was in trouble.

Under King Sennacherib, the mighty Assyrians had conquered the northern kingdom of Israel and were systematically advancing south, decimating the cities of Judea along the way. In an attempt to purchase peace, King Hezekiah paid his enemy an enormous tribute of gold and silver (2 Kings 18:14–16).

The ruthless Sennacherib repaid Hezekiah's subservience by ordering his armies to besiege the Judean capital. Through messengers he taunted the inhabitants: "Do not let your God in whom you trust deceive you by promising that Jerusalem will not be given into the hand of the king of Assyria. Behold, you have heard what the kings of Assyria have done to all lands, devoting them to destruction. And shall you be delivered?" (2 Kings 19:10–11).

Indeed, with such a massive army encircling the city, the situation seemed worse than bleak.

King Hezekiah and the Judeans prayed desperately for deliverance. Then, according

to 2 Kings 19:35, "the angel of the LORD went out and struck down 185,000 in the camp of the Assyrians."

For a long time many questioned the historicity and accuracy of this account. However, the famous Sennacherib Prism (a hexagonal clay artifact discovered at Nineveh in 1830) has raised eyebrows. Covered with Akkadian cuneiform writing, and dating to 690 BC, the artifact confirms Hezekiah's siege. And, because this record makes no mention of Jerusalem's capture, the general feeling among historians is that something indeed prevented Sennacherib from conquering the overmatched city. Had he overwhelmed the city, the thinking goes, surely his historians would have boasted about it.

Since pestilences were common in the ancient world, some theorize that the Assyrian army could have been stricken by a plague—perhaps cholera. We may never know what happened, but Sennacherib's army had no victory that day. ■

51 King Mesha Sacrifices His Firstborn Son

Why would an incident of child sacrifice by one of Israel's enemies result in trouble for Israel?

That's the mysterious situation recorded in 2 Kings 3. When the Moabite king Mesha revolted against King Jehoram of Israel, Jehoram responded by forming an alliance with King Jehoshaphat of Judah and the king of Edom. Together, they attacked Moab.

The author of 2 Kings wrote, "When the king of Moab saw that the battle was going against him, he took with him 700 swordsmen to break through, opposite the king of Edom, but they could not. Then he took his oldest son who was to reign in his place and offered him for

a burnt offering on the wall. And there came great wrath against Israel. And they withdrew from him and returned to their own land" (3:26–27).

Historical evidence shows that child sacrifice occurred in ancient times. A cuneiform tablet found in Syria, dating to the second millennium BC, describes the sacrifice of a child to the Canaanite god Baal in hopes of securing Baal's protection against an invading foe. Much later, Roman historians recounted similar incidents—including one where 200 children were put to death to forestall imminent defeat.

What we don't know is how to interpret the phrase "there came great wrath against Israel." Some think this means the Israelites were the target of the intense fury of the Moabites, who drove them from their land.

Others believe that the Judean troops of Jehoshaphat were sickened and angered when they witnessed the atrocity that resulted from Jehoram's invasion of Moab. ■

Above: Limestone stele of King Sennacherib from Nineveh. Ancient Orient Museum, Istanbul Archaeology Museums, Turkey. Photo by Osama Shukir Muhammed Amin FRCP (Glasg).

CHAPTER TEN

Between the Testaments

Caves of Qumran in Israel where the Dead Sea Scrolls were found.

(52) The Dead Sea Scrolls

In 1947, as the story is often told, an Arab shepherd boy tending his flock near the shores of the Dead Sea accidentally made one of the most important discoveries in the history of biblical scholarship. Searching for a lost goat, he is said to have tossed a stone into a cave. Instead of a bleat, he heard the sound of breaking pottery. Investigating, he discovered ancient scrolls hidden in clay pots.

Over the years almost a thousand manuscripts and tens of thousands of manuscript fragments were found in eleven caves in the cliffs along the desolate shoreline (a twelfth cave has recently been discovered).

Written predominantly in Hebrew, these "Dead Sea Scrolls" include writings in early paleo-Hebrew, Aramaic, and even Greek translations of the Hebrew Bible. They date from the third century BC to the first century AD. They include not only texts or fragments of nearly every book of the Hebrew Bible but also many valuable historical documents.

These scrolls have given the world the oldest surviving manuscripts of the Hebrew Bible. One nearly complete scroll of the book of Isaiah is a thousand years older than any other previously known copy! Extrabiblical scrolls include the bulky Temple Scroll, which is twenty-six feet long.

But who would have gone to such lengths to hide so many manuscripts in such an inhospitable location? In hopes of answering that question, attention focused on the nearby archaeological ruins of Qumran, which is believed to be the ancient settlement of a Jewish ascetical sect. Knowing they would be attacked and likely killed by the Romans during the Jewish-Roman War of AD 66–73, the inhabitants may have hid their precious manuscripts in nearby caves and abandoned the city. The dry climate preserved them for nearly 2,000 years. ■

Below: Dead Sea Scrolls on display at the caves of Qumran. They consist of biblical and extrabiblical manuscripts.

53 The Enigmatic Copper Scroll

The Dead Sea Scroll discoveries sparked an all-out search of desert caves in and around Qumran. In 1952, a most unusual item was found in what has come to be known as Qumran cave 3. Over in the shadows, separated from a stash of fragmented vellum scrolls, were two connected halves of a scroll made out of pure copper. Inscribed with Hebrew writing, this metallic manuscript measures eleven inches high and eight feet long.

Finding this rare artifact was thrilling. But the real excitement began when scholars deciphered its message. Can you believe the scroll lists sixty-four theoretical locations where supposedly 174 tons of gold, silver, and other valuables from the temple had once been hidden? Had archaeologists stumbled upon an actual treasure map to all sorts of biblical riches?

Many have heard this bizarre story of the Copper Scroll and cried, "Hoax!" If the scroll was meant to deceive, it's an expensive pretense (as copper was a high-priced commodity around the beginning of the Common Era). Also, who tries to start a ruse from a remote location that might never be found?

A few scholars (and more than a few adventurers) wasted no time in launching searches for this buried treasure. Yet, despite careful following of the detailed directions, no treasure has ever been found. ■

54 The Cave of Horror

Hidden in a cliff face near the southern end of the Dead Sea lies a cave containing shocking evidence of a desperate struggle that took place during the time "between the Testaments." The site, referred to by scholars as Nahal Hever cave 8, is some twenty-five miles south of the Qumran Caves and roughly nine miles north of Masada. It is called the Cave of Horror because the skeletons of about forty men, women, and children were found there.

Some scholars believe this tragedy occurred in AD 13 when the Second Jewish Revolt was being crushed by Roman legions. Those Jews who were able fled to remote, desolate regions in hopes of escaping their oppressors. The occupants of Nahal Hever cave 8 seem to have been well-to-do Jews, given the luxurious artifacts and letters found there.

Their elite status, however, could not save them. They were pursued by Roman troops, who set up siege camps on the heights above the cave. The Romans simply waited for their prey to run out of food and water.

As evidenced at Masada, the final few who remained alive may have committed suicide in order to avoid surrendering to the Romans. ■

Top: Qumran cave 3.
Bottom: View of Nahal Hever.

55 Masada

Overlooking the Dead Sea south of Qumran stands an impressive rock plateau—called Masada. This site was recognized by the ancients as a natural stronghold. Between 37 and 31 BC, King Herod the Great fortified the site, one of several fortresses the mistrustful ruler had built for himself. (Herod the Great was the paranoid king who, according to the Matthew 2:1–18, ordered the deaths of infants boys in Bethlehem when he heard the news of Jesus's birth.)

In AD 66 the people of Judea rebelled against Roman occupation, and four legions of Romans were tasked with crushing the revolt. As the Roman armies destroyed the countryside and attacked Jerusalem, Masada was soon crowded with hundreds of Judeans fleeing in search of a secure refuge.

In AD 72 the Romans, under the leadership of Lucius Flavius Silva Nonius Bassus, arrived at the base of Masada but found the steep cliff walls to be insurmountable. They then ringed the mountain with army camps to prevent any Judeans from escaping, and they set about building a massive siege ramp across a deep gorge to the summit.

As the siege ramp approached the cliff walls of Masada, the defenders began to hurl down rocks on their attackers. The Romans then brought Jewish slaves to continue the building, which left the besieged Judeans with an awful decision: either attack their fellow Jews laboring below or hold back and face the inevitable.

The Judeans on Masada made the fateful decision to spare their brethren. They paid the ultimate price when the site was about to be overthrown: rather than be slaughtered by the Romans, most of Masada's 960 defenders committed suicide. Only two women and five children survived (according to Josephus, *The Wars of the Jews*, book 7). ■

Above: Aerial view of Masada, Israel.

56 The Essene Sect

The New Testament mentions several Jewish sects: the Pharisees, the Sadducees, and the Zealots. One small historical sect not explicitly mentioned in the Bible was the Essenes. This group has greatly enhanced our knowledge of intertestamental Jewish life and politics. The Essenes renounced earthly possessions and sought to serve God through religious zeal and the strict adherence to the Sabbath laws.

The Essenes were believed to be followers of an enigmatic figure called the Teacher of Righteousness, who sought to bring spiritual renewal to the Jewish people. After losing a power struggle in Jerusalem, in which their leader may have been killed, the Essenes withdrew from society to the remote shores of the Dead Sea.

Among the scrolls (now known as the Dead Sea Scrolls) secreted in caves near their community was a document that described a future war at the end of the age between "the Sons of Light" and the "Sons of Darkness." According to this writing, this final battle will be won by divine intervention, with the victorious righteous enjoying a messianic age of peace.

The apocalyptic teachings of the Essenes doubtlessly influenced zealous Jews in the time leading up to the First Jewish Revolt. The Judeans revolted against Roman occupation, believing that God would intervene on their behalf. Unfortunately, the culminating battle they sought did not materialize. Rome was victorious, and the Essenes disappeared from the pages of history. ■

Above: Qumran, where the Dead Sea Scrolls were found, Israel.

57 An Age of Messiahs

Both the New Testament and the Jewish historian Josephus mention the messianic fervor that permeated Israel in the first century.

The followers of John the Baptist, for example, wondered whether he, a fiery preacher of righteousness dressed in camel skin, might be the one spoken of by the Jewish prophets. John shut down all such talk, "He came right out and said, 'I am not the Messiah' " (John 1:20, NLT). In the Gospel of Luke, John says, "I baptize you with water, but he who is mightier than I is coming, the strap of whose sandals I am not worthy to untie" (Luke 3:16).

In Acts 5, we read the words of a Pharisee named Gamaliel about another would-be Messiah. "Some time ago Theudas appeared, claiming to be somebody, and about four hundred men rallied to him. He was killed, all his followers were dispersed, and it all came to nothing" (verse 36, NIV).

This incident happened during the rule of the Roman procurator Cuspius Fadus (AD 44–46). Josephus reported that Theudas led his followers to the Jordan River, where he attempted to perform miracles. Cuspius Fadus dispatched soldiers, who then killed Theudas and arrested many of his followers.

But he remained silent and made no answer. Again the high priest asked him, "Are you the Christ, the Son of the Blessed?" And Jesus said, "I am, and you will see the Son of Man seated at the right hand of Power, and coming with the clouds of heaven." And the high priest tore his garments and said, "What further witnesses do we need?

MARK 14:61–63

Josephus also mentioned an Egyptian who led thousands of disciples to the Mount of Olives during the time of the procurator Felix (AD 52–59). In the book of Acts, Paul is accused of being this man: "Are you not the Egyptian, then, who recently stirred up a revolt and led the four thousand men of the Assassins out into the wilderness?" (21:38). Unlike Jesus, who humbly entered Jerusalem riding a donkey, the unnamed Egyptian boasted that he would break down the walls of Jerusalem and enter the city as a king. Also unlike Jesus, the Egyptian escaped as Roman soldiers killed 400 of his followers.

Given all this, it's not surprising, then, to read in the Gospels that some people were excited and others worried by talk about Jesus being the Messiah (Mark 14:61–63; John 1:41–42, 4:29–30). ■

Above: The romanticized woodcut engraving of Flavius Josephus appearing in William Whiston's translation of his works.

CHAPTER ELEVEN

Herod the Great

View from Masada, King Herod's fortress.

+SCS BALTHASSAR +SCS MELCHIOR +SCS GASPAR.

58 The Year of Jesus's Birth

Details provided in the Gospels help historians date the birth of Jesus.

The Gospel of Luke informs us that Jesus was born "in the days of Herod, king of Judea" (1:5). This Herod, commonly known as Herod the Great, ruled Judea between 37 BC and AD 4. He is not to be confused with the "Herod the tetrarch," known as Herod Antipas, referred to in Matthew 14:1. Antipas was one of the three sons of Herod the Great. He reigned over Galilee and Perea from AD 4 to 39, meaning he was still in power when Jesus was tried, condemned, and crucified.

Since Herod the Great was alive when Jesus was born in Bethlehem, this means Jesus could not have been born later than AD 4. Furthermore, since this Herod died when Jesus was still very young—and in exile in Egypt (Matthew 2:19–21)—Jesus must have been born some time before 4 BC.

The Gospel of Matthew confirms this. It tells us Herod received "wise men from the east" and learned from them of the birth in Bethlehem of one who had "been born king of the Jews" (2:1–2). Determined to remove any possible threat to his throne, Herod "killed all the male children in Bethlehem and in all that region who were two years old or under, according to the time that he had ascertained from the wise men" (Matthew 2:16). Herod's calculations suggest a birth date between 6 and 5 BC. ◼

Above: Three kings bearing gifts for Jesus. Ancient UNESCO-listed Byzantine mosaic from Ravenna, Italy.

59 Herod the Great

Herod ruled Judea for more than three decades and left his indelible mark upon the nation. He was not of Jewish heritage. The infamous monarch, who bestowed upon himself the title "Herod the Great," hailed from Idumea, south of Judea.

Herod had been appointed governor of Galilee, but he fled to Rome in 41 BC when he was threatened by a coup attempt. While there, Herod managed to win the favor of Emperor Octavian. Proclaimed king of the Jews by the Roman Senate, Herod returned to Judea—backed by the full power and authority of Judea's Roman occupiers—and in three years managed to subdue the land.

Herod was disliked by many of his subjects. They resented the high taxes he levied on them to pay for his lavish building projects. They abhorred his impiety. Herod ruthlessly suppressed any perceived threat to his rule—the most notorious biblical example being the slaughter of the infants of Bethlehem in an attempt to eliminate the newborn "king of the Jews" (Matthew 2:2, 16).

As the end of his life drew near, Herod was determined that people across the land would mourn for him. He summoned a large number of dignitaries to his palace in Jericho and gave orders that upon his death they be put to death—a command that thankfully was not carried out. ∎

60 Judea under Roman Rule

Beginning in 722 BC the people and land of Israel were subjugated by a series of foreign powers: the Assyrians, Babylonians, Persians, and Greeks. In 165 BC, Jewish rebels threw off the yoke of their oppressors and established the independent Hasmonean kingdom. This exercise in self-governance lasted only a century before Judea was torn apart by civil war.

In 63 BC, the Roman general Pompey was leading a military campaign in the East and decided to consolidate Roman rule in the eastern Mediterranean region. After the sacking of Jerusalem, Judea was incorporated into the Roman province of Syria. In 41 BC Rome installed the Idumean Herod the Great as ruler.

Ten years after Herod's death, Judea became a Roman province governed by procurators, the most famous of whom, Pontius Pilate, presided over the crucifixion of Jesus. In the ensuing decades Jewish resistance to the occupying Romans intensified. This culminated in the First Jewish Revolt in AD 66. Despite grievous losses and a crushing defeat at the hands of the Roman legions, some seventy years later the Jews revolted again, under the leadership of Simon Bar Kokhba.

Once again the Romans committed overwhelming force to crush the rebellion. It would take the better part of two millennia before the age-old yearning of the Jewish people for a sovereign state would become a reality. ∎

Top: Inscription of Herod the Great. Year and artist unknown.
Bottom: Herodion (or the Herodium), fortress of Herod the Great, Judean desert, Israel.

61 Herod's Magnificent Building Projects

When Herod the Great was appointed king of Judea by the Roman Senate, he was granted wide powers to remake Judea in his own image. Herod was faced with two irreconcilable goals: currying favor with his Jewish subjects while at the same time seeking to please the Romans, who kept him in power.

Accordingly, Herod embarked upon an ambitious construction program across the land that was intended to impress his Roman patrons and win the respect of the Jews, while establishing his legacy for generations to come. His splendid new city, Caesarea Maritime, was the pride of the eastern Mediterranean lands. The city boasted a state-of-the-art port, a theater, a hippodrome, administrative buildings, sumptuous villas, and an aqueduct. To the dismay of devout Jews, the city also included a pagan temple dedicated to Caesar.

Herod also rebuilt the walls of Jerusalem along with theaters, markets, and palaces. His crowning achievement, however, was the rebuilding of the Jewish temple on an imposing scale. It is recorded that ten thousand skilled craftsmen were employed in the massive project, which was one of the larger building projects of its time anywhere in the Roman world.

The temple also featured a golden eagle—the symbol of Roman power—prominently situated over the entranceway, an unthinkable sacrilege in the eyes of the devout. Herod's subservience to Judea's hated occupiers doomed his relations with his Jewish subjects. ■

Ruins at Caesarea Maritime.

CHAPTER TWELVE

A King Is Born

Mary, Joseph, and Jesus, Nativity Church, Bethlehem, Israel.

62 No Room at the Inn

Did you know that many of our Christmas programs and Nativity scenes feature some details not actually found in the Bible?

Only two of the four Gospels—Matthew and Luke—contain infancy narratives of Jesus. Luke tells of Mary and Joseph traveling to Bethlehem to register for a census decreed by Caesar Augustus (2:1–4). Neither Gospel says anything about Mary riding a donkey. Neither specifically mentions an innkeeper. Luke simply says that when Mary and Joseph tried to find lodging in Bethlehem "there was no place for them in the inn" (2:7). We assume if there was an inn, there must have been an innkeeper; however, we don't actually read about such a person in the Gospels.

Though Luke doesn't explicitly mention a "stable," we know that when Mary gave birth to Jesus she "wrapped him in swaddling cloths and laid him in a manger" (2:7). A manger is a feeding trough for animals—although no animals are overtly mentioned in Luke 2:6–7, which describes the scene of Jesus's birth. It's from this mention of a manger that we assume Jesus was born in some sort of shelter for animals. This shelter was almost certainly *not* like a modern barn or stable or shed. In fact, Palestinian homes of that era were often built over natural caves where a family's animals could find shelter. So, it's entirely possible that a shallow cave served as the humble birthplace of the baby Jesus.

Luke's account focuses on the night of the birth. He talks only about shepherds. If wise men were at the manger, Luke doesn't mention them.

Matthew's account seems to pick up the story some time later—a few days or possibly even a few weeks. He specifically mentions Mary and the child being in a "house" (Matthew 2:11). He doesn't mention shepherds being at the "house." He—and he alone—talks about the visit of the wise men. Matthew says nothing about the wise men riding camels. He never calls them kings, and he never says there were three. We assume they were three in number because they presented three gifts to Jesus. ■

Above: *The Adoration of the Shepherds* (ca. 1460) by Andrea Mantegna (1431–1506).

63 The Wise Men and the Star

The first Gospel says that after Jesus was born "wise men from the East came to Jerusalem, saying, 'Where is He who has been born King of the Jews? For we have seen His star in the East and have come to worship Him'" (Matthew 2:1–2, NKJV).

Scholars, scientists, and clergy have speculated endlessly about what this passage is actually saying. What star or constellation or heavenly sign might these wise men, or *magi* (the word suggests they were astrologers, probably from Persia or Babylonia), have seen that prompted them to undertake such a long, dangerous journey?

The astronomer Johannes Kepler (AD 1471–1630) calculated that three alignments of Jupiter and Saturn occurred in the constellation Pisces in 7 BC. Even more momentous was an alignment of Mars, Jupiter, and Saturn in September of 6 BC—a rare event that occurs only once every 800 years.

Chinese astronomers identified a new star in the constellation Capricorn that was visible for seventy days in 5 BC.

Some have suggested these learned men may have actually had access to copies of the Torah, thanks to the Jews who remained in Babylonia following the exile. If so, the speculation goes, perhaps their reference to a star stems from the prophecy found in Numbers 24:17, which says, "A star will come out of Jacob; a scepter will rise out of Israel" (NIV).

The biggest mystery is that these wise men (plural, so we know there were at least two) departed Jerusalem and, according to the Gospel of Matthew, "the star which they had seen in the East went before them, till it came and stood over where the young Child was" (2:9, NKJV).

This sounds so detailed and specific, almost like these Eastern visitors had a heavenly laser pointer guiding them. However this star "went before them," Matthew says it led them to where Jesus was. ■

64 Slaughter of the Innocents

When Herod the Great learned of the birth of Jesus in Bethlehem, he attempted to enlist the visiting wise men to find out where this newborn "king" was (Matthew 2:1–8). When the wise men refused to play along and did not return to him, Herod flew into a rage. "He sent forth and put to death all the male children who were in Bethlehem and in all its districts, from two years old and under, according to the time which he had determined from the wise men" (Matthew 2:16, NKJV).

Some wonder if this atrocity is fanciful or historical. Let's say this: ordering the mass murder of Bethlehem's baby boys is consistent with other violent acts attributed to Herod.

During his final years, Herod became extremely paranoid. On one occasion he executed 300 military leaders for suspected disloyalty. On another, a group of Pharisees were killed for predicting his downfall.

At one time historians estimated the number of slaughtered innocents to be in the thousands. More recent evidence, however, suggests that Bethlehem was a small town or large village at the time of Jesus's birth, suggesting a lesser number of children. ■

Above: *Slaughter of the Innocents* (1304–1306) by Giotto (1266–1337), Scrovegni Chapel, Padua, Italy.

65 Death of a Tyrant

Herod the Great's rule was characterized by a brutality that was exceptional even for the standards of the day. He ruthlessly exterminated any suspected threats to his regime. He killed his father-in-law in a cruel act of political expediency. Several of his wives and three of his sons also fell under his ax. Emperor Augustus fittingly jested in a play on words that it would be better to be Herod's pig (Greek: *hus*) than his son (*huios*).

Herod's final days, however, serve as a reminder of the old saying "A man reaps what he sows" (Galatians 6:7, NIV). The Jewish historian Josephus recorded that Herod suffered some sort of excruciating intestinal disease. Desperate for a cure, Herod had himself carefully transported to his palace in Jericho. He hoped to benefit from the nearby hot springs—to no avail.

Eager to assume the throne, Herod's ambitious son Antipater made the devastating mistake of rejoicing at the premature news that his father had died. When word reached the temporarily revived Herod, he immediately had Antipater executed.

Josephus wrote that shortly afterward, Herod suffered an agonizing death involving burning fever, ulcerated entrails, foul discharges, and convulsions (*Antiquities of the Jews*, 17.6.5). Perhaps this condition was genetic? Josephus also recorded how Herod's grandson Herod Agrippa met a similar fate in the amphitheater at Caesarea Maritime. After Agrippa stepped into the theater wearing a silver, shimmering garment, "his flatterers cried out that he was a god; and they added, 'Be thou merciful to us; for although we have hitherto reverenced thee only as a man, yet shall we henceforth own thee as superior to mortal nature.' Upon this the king did neither rebuke them, nor reject their impious flattery." Josephus then recorded Agrippa being struck with pain in his belly and passing five days later. Or, as recorded in the book of Acts, "Immediately, because Herod did not give praise to God, an angel of the Lord struck him down, and he was eaten by worms and died" (12:23, NIV). ∎

66 Where Is Herod's Tomb?

The Jewish historian Josephus recorded that after Herod the Great died in 4 BC, his body was placed on a golden and bejeweled bier, covered in royal purple. Accompanied by a multitude of family, servants, and soldiers, Herod's remains were transported in a majestic funeral procession to the Herodium, where he was buried.

Herod named the Herodium after himself; it was one of his most impressive building projects, constructed as a refuge in case the hated ruler was ever forced to flee Jerusalem. The towering fortress was the tallest peak in the Judean desert. Four massive towers atop the steep hillside guarded against intruders. A palace on the summit was equipped with a Roman bathhouse and theater, banquet rooms, and lavish living quarters.

Eventually the site was abandoned and remained undisturbed until the nineteenth century, when archaeologists searched in vain for Herod's tomb on the Herodium. In 2007, after over a century of searching, prominent Israeli archaeologist Ehud Netzer announced that his team had uncovered the burial crypt.

Amid all the excitement, few noticed that compared with other royal sepulchres of the era, the tomb was far too modest for a potentate such as Herod. Did Herod design a small, hidden burial site to prevent his enemies from discovering and pillaging his tomb? Or does a grandiose mausoleum bearing Herod's remains still lie undisturbed in the Judean desert? ∎

Above: Herod's tomb in Herodion, photo courtesy of Deror avi.

67 Jesus's Missing Years

The Gospels contain a puzzling omission: there are no explicit mentions of what Jesus did between the ages of twelve (Luke 2:41–51) and thirty (Luke 3:23).

There has been no shortage of theories advanced to account for these "lost years." Assorted speculations have Jesus visiting numerous countries on several continents during this time.

One claim is that Jesus journeyed to the Himalayas, where he trained with Buddhist monks. A supposed third-century AD manuscript describing his years there has never materialized. If this hypothesis is true, one would expect Jesus's teachings to have an Eastern mystical flavor. However, his words reflect an uncompromising devotion to the Hebrew Bible.

Other theorists postulate that Jesus traveled to what is now Great Britain, where he was known as "Eisu." Similarly, residents of Shingō, Japan, refer to their village as *Kirisuto no Sato* ("Christ's Hometown") and claim that a twenty-one-year-old Jesus became a disciple of a Buddhist monk there. There is no credible evidence for any of these claims.

Yet another unsubstantiated theory suggests that Jesus joined the Essene sect, which settled near the Dead Sea.

The Gospels provide a strong clue as to how Jesus occupied his time between the ages of twelve and thirty. The people of Nazareth referred to him as "the carpenter's son" (Matthew 13:55) and "the carpenter" (Mark 6:3). The clear implication is that he likely learned woodworking from his stepfather, Joseph, while living and working in Nazareth. ∎

And when Jesus had finished these parables, he went away from there, and coming to his hometown he taught them in their synagogue, so that they were astonished, and said, "Where did this man get this wisdom and these mighty works? Is not this the carpenter's son? Is not his mother called Mary? And are not his brothers James and Joseph and Simon and Judas? And are not all his sisters with us? Where then did this man get all these things?"

MATTHEW 13:53–56

CHAPTER THIRTEEN

Ministry in Galilee

The Sermon on the Mount by Fra Angelico (1395–1455).

68 Is This the House of Peter?

The Gospel of Matthew tells of Jesus being in Capernaum (8:5) and says when he "entered Peter's house, he saw [Peter's] mother-in-law lying sick with a fever. He touched her hand, and the fever left her, and she rose and began to serve him" (8:14–15).

Is it possible that excavations in Capernaum have uncovered the actual site of this miracle?

Underneath the foundation of an eight-sided Byzantine church archaeologists have uncovered a very ordinary home with a roof made of earth and straw. It dates to the first century AD. At least six layers of plastered walls and pavement have been found, indicating that the area was preserved for an extended period of time.

Historians tell us that by the fourth century this house was apparently being used for religious gatherings.

More than one hundred bits of graffiti have been found on the walls—the names of Jesus, God, and Christ, as well as liturgical expressions and prayers like "Christ have mercy."

The Spanish sister Egeria wrote in AD 384 that the house of "the prince of the apostles" had become a church. By the sixth century the church was replaced by an impressive basilica—or pilgrimage site—the remains of which continue to draw tourists to the fishing village on the shores of the Sea of Galilee that Jesus called home during his adult years.

This circumstantial evidence doesn't prove this site is the actual house of Peter, but it does prompt this question: Why else would a simple home in this town have become a prominent gathering place for ancient Christians and pilgrims? ∎

The traditional home of St. Peter located in Capernaum.

69 The Gates of Hell

In the Gospel of Matthew, we read that Jesus journeyed with his disciples to the district of Caesarea Philippi in the far north of Judea, where he posed the question: "Who do people say that the Son of Man is?" (16:13). An examination of the history behind Caesarea Philippi could perhaps help us understand why Jesus would have queried his disciples at this important site.

The original name of the site was Panias, after the Greek god Pan, who is strongly associated with revelry and the unbridled pursuit of pleasure. Many ancient depictions of Pan show him engaging in sexual acts with humans as well as goats. A niche carved into the cliff walls once prominently displayed his statue, which has long since been removed.

Next to the now-empty niche is a massive cave from which a spring-fed stream issues. The cave—believed by some people to be the gates of hell—was once dedicated to Baal, lord of the underworld and of the dead. Baal was believed to descend to Hades each winter and ascend in spring via this cave.

Caesarea Philippi was regarded as the most pagan site in all of Judea. It is interesting that here Peter confessed to Jesus, "You are the Christ, the Son of the living God." Notice Jesus's reply: "You are Peter, and on this rock I will build my church, and the gates of hell shall not prevail against it" (Matthew 16:16, 18). ∎

He said to them, "But who do you say that I am?" Simon Peter replied, "You are the Christ, the Son of the living God." And Jesus answered him, "Blessed are you, Simon Bar-Jonah! For flesh and blood has not revealed this to you, but my Father who is in heaven. And I tell you, you are Peter, and on this rock I will build my church, and the gates of hell shall not prevail against it. I will give you the keys of the kingdom of heaven, and whatever you bind on earth shall be bound in heaven, and whatever you loose on earth shall be loosed in heaven." Then he strictly charged the disciples to tell no one that he was the Christ.

MATTHEW 16:15–20

Top Right: Panias.
Bottom Left: Carved niches in the Temple of Pan wall.

70 Jesus and the Demon-Possessed Man

The Gospel of Mark relates an encounter between Jesus and a man described as being possessed by a "legion of demons" (5:15, NIV). All attempts to restrain him had failed: "For he had often been chained hand and foot, but he tore the chains apart and broke the irons on his feet" (5:4, NIV).

After Jesus commanded the evil spirits to depart, they begged to be sent into a nearby herd of pigs, after which "the herd, about two thousand in number, rushed down the steep bank into the lake and were drowned" (Mark 5:13, NIV).

People have questioned the validity of this story for two reasons: (1) Why would such a large herd of ritually unclean pigs have been grazing in Judea? (2) The terrain around the Sea of Galilee doesn't feature cliffs.

The answer to the first question is found in the book of Mark which records that Jesus and his disciples had gone "across the lake to the region of the Gerasenes" (Mark 5:1, NIV).

As far as the second question, we know that the topography of landforms can change over time. In 1985, after a prolonged drought caused the Sea of Galilee's waterline to drop, a large harbor was discovered. Near this ancient harbor is a site where a cliff (that is usually underwater) overlooks the lake and could fit the Gospel description.

According to Mark's Gospel, the inhabitants of the region did not appreciate losing their livelihood; they asked Jesus to leave their territory. The man who had been delivered from the demons, however, proved to be a faithful witness. When Jesus returned to the Decapolis a year and a half later, at least 4,000 people were eagerly awaiting him (Mark 7:31–8:10). ∎

They came to the other side of the sea, to the country of the Gerasenes. And when Jesus had stepped out of the boat, immediately there met him out of the tombs a man with an unclean spirit. He lived among the tombs.

MARK 5:1–3

Above: South gate of Gerasa.

CHAPTER FOURTEEN

Jewish Sects and Schisms

Christ Healing the Blind Men on the Road to Jericho by Pieter Norbert van Reysschoot (1738–1795).

71 Second-Class Citizens

On his way to Jerusalem, Jesus was approached by a group of ten men suffering from leprosy. Because of their sickness, and the requirement that they remain in isolation, these lepers called out to Jesus from a distance. In healing them, Jesus instructed them to go show themselves to the priests. This was in accordance with the Mosaic Law, which mandated that people healed of leprosy first present themselves for examination.

We read that "one of them, when he saw that he was healed, turned back, praising God with a loud voice; and he fell on his face at Jesus' feet, giving him thanks. Now he was a Samaritan" (Luke 17:15–16). Jesus took this opportunity to bless this man who was only partly Jewish. Such an act would have offended many first-

century Jews who despised Samaritans as second-class citizens. Why?

Most scholars believe that the Samaritans descended from the intermarriages of Jews and Gentiles—perhaps in the wake of the Assyrian defeat of the northern kingdom of Israel, seven centuries before the time of Jesus. Pure-blooded Jews despised and avoided the Samaritans, who were of mixed ancestry.

Jesus addressed this kind of prideful attitude in the parable of the Good Samaritan. That story shows two of the most respected figures in Jewish life—a priest and a Levite—refusing to help a man left for dead along the road. It is a Samaritan who binds up the man's wounds and spares no expense in assisting him (see Luke 10:25–37).

72 The Separated Ones

The Pharisees were respected as teachers and interpreters of Jewish law. They exercised considerable influence over the two central Jewish institutions: the synagogue and the Sanhedrin, or religious court. The name *Pharisee* likely refers to "separated ones"—those who isolate themselves from society and practice ritual purity.

Some scholars, such as historian Paul Johnson, believe that the Pharisees were a sect formed out of opposition to Greek rulers and Hellenistic culture, beginning about 170 BC. In 167 BC, the Greeks dismissed the Mosaic Law as a guide for civic life and turned the Jewish temple into a place of ecumenical worship. In opposition to Greek education, pious Jews developed their own system of education, which Johnson says helped give birth to separatist notions in Pharisaism.

Another possible reason for the Pharisees' separation from a cultural context occurred later, in about 100 BC. As they formed themselves into a religious party, they opposed the Sadducees, an aristocratic Jewish sect that supported royal alliances with Rome.

In the first century AD, the Pharisees were known for scrupulous devotion to tithing and to the Jewish law. The Gospels show that despite the Pharisees' fierce commitment to observe Jewish rituals and customs, they were frequently criticized by Jesus. On one occasion, he said to them: "Woe to you, teachers of the law and Pharisees, you hypocrites! You give a tenth of your spices—mint, dill and cumin. But you have neglected the more important matters of the law—justice, mercy and faithfulness. You should have practiced the latter, without neglecting the former" (Matthew 23:23, NIV). ∎

Above: *Supper in the House of Simon the Pharisee* by Romanino (ca. 1484–1562).

73 Judean Freedom Fighters

Unlike other Jewish sects that either grudgingly accepted Roman rule or dramatically withdrew from society, the Zealots advocated revolt against foreign occupation. Believing that Judeans must submit to God alone, they refused to pay taxes or acknowledge the authority of their Roman overlords.

Surprisingly, "Simon the Zealot" (Matthew 10:4) is listed as one of Jesus's handpicked disciples, although we learn nothing more about him.

Then at Jesus's trial, we meet another who shared the philosophy of the Zealots. We read that "a man called Barabbas was in prison with the insurrectionists who had committed murder in the uprising" (Mark 15:7, NIV). These "insurrectionists" were likely allied with the Zealots, and they apparently enjoyed the favor of the people—because when given a choice between Jesus and Barabbas, "the whole crowd shouted, 'Away with this man! Release Barabbas to us!' " (Luke 23:18, NIV).

In the decades after Jesus, the Zealots' opposition to Rome grew increasingly bold, and they played a central role in the First Jewish Revolt in AD 66. As the revolt was being crushed by the Roman legions, the Zealots who refused to admit defeat executed those who counseled surrender. As Jerusalem was surrounded and set ablaze, the last remnant of the Zealots escaped to the desert fortress of Masada, where they made one last, futile stand. ∎

Now at the feast he used to release for them one prisoner for whom they asked. And among the rebels in prison, who had committed murder in the insurrection, there was a man called Barabbas. And the crowd came up and began to ask Pilate to do as he usually did for them. . . . But the chief priests stirred up the crowd to have him release for them Barabbas instead.
MARK 15:6–8, 11

Above: *Give Us Barabbas,* from *The Bible and Its Story Taught by One Thousand Picture Lessons.* This work is in the public domain in the United States.

74 The Herodians

We read in the Gospel of Mark how "the Pharisees . . . plotted with the Herodians against [Jesus], how they might destroy Him" (Mark 3:6, NKJV). The Herodians were opposed to Jesus for political reasons, and the Pharisees opposed him for religious reasons. So began the scheming between two political groups that formerly were enemies that would culminate in Jesus's crucifixion.

In Mark 12, we see an example of the Pharisees and the Herodians scheming against Jesus. A group of them came to Jesus and said, "Teacher, we know that you are true and do not care about anyone's opinion. For you are not swayed by appearances, but truly teach the way of God. Is it lawful to pay taxes to Caesar, or not?" (verse 14).

On its face, their question sounds sincere. It was not. These Pharisees and Herodians were sent specifically to "trap [Jesus] in his talk" (Mark 12:13). The question was a sly attempt to get Jesus to say something that would enrage either the masses or those in power. As their name suggests, the Herodians were loyal supporters of Herod Antipas. It is not known why they maintained such devotion to this puppet-king who reigned only in a limited way under the watchful eye of Rome. Perhaps they shared family ties?

As trick questions go, this one was brilliant. If Jesus encouraged the payment of taxes, he would offend the majority of the populace that bitterly resented the Roman occupation. On the other hand, Antipas would be keenly interested to know if the Nazarene teacher advocated some kind of tax revolt.

Jesus's reply amazed and silenced his questioners: "Render to Caesar the things that are Caesar's, and to God the things that are God's" (Mark 12:17). ■

Top: Coin of Tiberius (ca. AD 27–30).
Bottom: Illustration of Jesus and the story of the tribute money.

75 The Worldly Minded Aristocrats

The Hebrew word for **Sadducees** means "righteous ones," a reference to the group's claim to be descendants of Zadok, the high priest in the days of Solomon. In first-century Judea, the Sadducees oversaw the temple and the daily sacrifices, and they were heavily represented in the Jewish court, or Sanhedrin.

Because the Sadducees cultivated good relations with the political ruling powers, they enjoyed great influence in both civil and religious matters. They jealously guarded this privileged position and were power brokers in Judea. The first-century historian Josephus, fairly or not, described them as elitist and boorish.

The New Testament Gospels present the Sadducees as vehemently opposed to Jesus. Mark tells of one incident in which these deniers of the immortality of the soul attempted to ensnare Jesus with a complicated question about marriage in the resurrection. Jesus sidestepped their trap by quoting from the Torah, the only part of the Hebrew Bible this group claimed to believe (Mark 12:18–27).

The Sadducees and rival Pharisees are often presented in the Gospels as uniting together to challenge the words and works of Jesus. Clearly, it's not just politics that makes for strange bedfellows. ■

Above: *The Question of the Sadducees* by Harold Copping (1863–1932).

CHAPTER FIFTEEN

Events in Judea

The Calling of the Apostles Peter and Andrew (ca. 1308–1311) by Duccio di Buoninsegna (ca. 1255–ca. 1319).

76 The Pinnacle of the Temple

We can understand the temptation to eat when you haven't had a bite in six weeks or to take a shortcut to power. But what right-minded person feels inclined to jump off a building?

According to the Gospel of Luke, after fasting for forty days in the wilderness, Jesus endured three great temptations at the hand of Satan. In the first, Satan taunted Jesus to make bread out of stones. Jesus replied: "It is written, 'Man shall not live by bread alone' " (Luke 4:4).

Satan then took Jesus to a high mountain, where he offered him all the earthly kingdoms if only he would bow the knee to Satan. Jesus responded by quoting from Deuteronomy: "It is written, 'You shall worship the Lord your God, and him only shall you serve' " (Luke 4:8).

Finally, Satan took Jesus atop the temple, and urged him to throw himself down. Satan said, "For it is written, 'He will command his angels concerning you, to guard you' " (Luke 4:10).

It seems ludicrous to us, but perhaps this was the most compelling of the three temptations. Jesus knew the Hebrew Bible well, and perhaps he knew that the people in the temple courts below would likely recall Malachi's ancient prophecy concerning the Messiah: "And the Lord whom you seek will suddenly come to his temple" (Malachi 3:1). Yet, Jesus resisted, quoting again from Deuteronomy: "You shall not put the Lord your God to the test" (Luke 4:12). ∎

Above: *Temptation of Jesus*, Saint George Church, Antwerp, Belgium.

77 Woe to the Man: A Study in Betrayal

What do we know—really—about Judas Iscariot, the disciple who betrayed Jesus? In truth, not a lot. However, an incident portrayed in the Gospel of John provides insight into his enigmatic character.

When Mary anointed Jesus's feet with expensive perfume, Judas protested loudly, "Why wasn't this perfume sold and the money given to the poor? It was worth a year's wages" (John 12:5, NIV). His argument sounds so noble. But John lets us know that Judas's "concern" was a mask to disguise his own greed and dishonesty: "He did not say this because he cared about the poor but because he was a thief; as keeper of the money bag, he used to help himself to what was put into it" (John 12:6, NIV).

Judas's avarice became full-blown when he approached the chief priests, offering to betray Jesus: " 'What will you give me if I deliver him over to you?' And they paid him thirty pieces of silver" (Matthew 26:15).

Some have theorized that Judas was only trying to force Jesus's hand—that by arranging a confrontation with the Roman officials and Jewish religious leaders he was perhaps hoping to get Jesus to begin a messianic revolution. Whether this is true or not, we will likely never know. We do know that Judas was overwhelmed with regret and despair after Jesus's crucifixion. He "went out and hanged himself" (Matthew 27:5, NLT).

The Gospel of Matthew states that when Jesus celebrated the Passover in Jerusalem with his disciples, he indicated that one of them would forsake him. Then he added this chilling statement: "But woe to that man by whom the Son of Man is betrayed! It would have been better for that man if he had not been born" (Matthew 26:24). ■

Above: Painting depicting Jesus and his disciples in the garden of Gethsemane when he was betrayed by Judas.

78 A Notorious Roman Procurator

After Judea came under direct Roman rule in AD 6, the newly formed province was governed by a series of prefects, or provincial governors. Pontius Pilate was the fifth prefect, ruling from AD 26 to 36.

Pilate soon offended his Jewish subjects. Unlike his predecessors, he ordered that images of Caesar, known as standards, be brought to Jerusalem and publicly displayed. This outraged devout Jews, who considered such depictions to be idolatry. Pilate's response was to have a group of them rounded up and threatened with execution if they did not cease their protests.

To his amazement, instead of meekly submitting, the Jews defiantly bared their necks, preferring to die rather than accept this sacrilege against their religion. Taken aback, Pilate ordered that the standards be removed from Jerusalem.

Opposition to Pilate was stirred up again when he raided the temple treasury to finance the building of an aqueduct. This time he was ready when the Jews protested. Soldiers disguised in civilian clothing mixed with the crowd, and at Pilate's signal they killed many of the protesters with swords.

A few years after presiding over the crucifixion of Jesus, Pilate finally went too far. After he ruthlessly attacked Samaritans who were wrongfully accused of fomenting revolt, they appealed to his superior in Syria. Pilate was ordered to Rome to give an account—and soon disappeared from history. ■

The inscription reads:

This building – Tiberium
By Pontius Pilatus
Prefect of Judea
Has been built

Top: Ruins of an ancient Caesarean residence of Pontius Pilate.
Bottom: The Pilate Inscription from Caesarea Maritima, Israel. Photo courtesy of Marion Doss.

Above: *Ecce Homo* by Antonio Ciseri (1821–1891).

79 The Raising of Lazarus

In the Gospel of John we read, "Now a man named Lazarus was sick. He was from Bethany, the village of Mary and her sister Martha" (11:1, NIV). Even though Jesus was only a day's journey from his ill friend, he waited until three days after Lazarus died before going to Bethany.

According to Jewish tradition, a dead person's spirit hovers over the body for three days before departing (perhaps this idea arose after some who were thought to be dead spontaneously revived). Writing that Jesus did not arrive until the fourth day after Lazarus's death would avoid any thought that Lazarus was not yet truly dead.

Approaching the tomb, "Jesus called in a loud voice, 'Lazarus, come out!' The dead man came out, his hands and feet wrapped with strips of linen, and a cloth around his face. Jesus said to them, 'Take off the grave clothes and let him go' " (John 11:43–44, NIV).

Archaeological excavations at the site of Bethany (near Jerusalem) have uncovered a fourth-century church built over a tomb thought to belong to Lazarus. ∎

Then Jesus, deeply moved again, came to the tomb. It was a cave, and a stone lay against it. Jesus said, "Take away the stone." Martha, the sister of the dead man, said to him, "Lord, by this time there will be an odor, for he has been dead four days." Jesus said to her, "Did I not tell you that if you believed you would see the glory of God?" So they took away the stone. And Jesus lifted up his eyes and said, "Father, I thank you that you have heard me. I knew that you always hear me, but I said this on account of the people standing around, that they may believe that you sent me." When he had said these things, he cried out with a loud voice, "Lazarus, come out." The man who had died came out, his hands and feet bound with linen strips, and his face wrapped with a cloth. Jesus said to them, "Unbind him, and let him go."

JOHN 11:38–44

Above Left: *Raising Lazarus*, fresco in Saint Nicholas's Cathedral, Ljubljana, Slovenia.

CHAPTER SIXTEEN

Jesus's Crucifixion

The Road to Calvary (1526) by Lorenzo Lotto (1480–1557).

80 The Most Wretched of Deaths

Mark 15:34 tells us that Jesus was crucified by the Roman authorities, but the punishment is not described in the biblical text. Crucifixion was a tortuous and humiliating form of execution. The Jewish historian Josephus aptly called it "the most wretched of deaths."

It was typically carried out at a prominent location, no doubt to strike fear into the hearts of the people. In first-century Jerusalem, Golgotha was such a site. This hill, said to resemble a skull, the actual meaning of the name, overlooked a major thoroughfare. When Jesus was crucified there, the Bible says that "those who passed by hurled insults at him, shaking their heads" (Matthew 27:39, NIV).

After being condemned by Pilate, Jesus was stripped and flogged. His hands were nailed to a crossbar, which was then hoisted up and secured to a vertical post.

In order to breathe, crucifixion victims had no choice but to push against the spikes that pierced their feet. Such movements were agonizing, but no other way existed for a crucified person to raise their torso high enough to gulp a bit of air. This sadistic experience sometimes went on for days, as the condemned slowly expired from exhaustion, dehydration, and suffocation.

And when they had crucified him, they divided his garments among them by casting lots. Then they sat down and kept watch over him there. And over his head they put the charge against him, which read, "This is Jesus, the King of the Jews." Then two robbers were crucified with him, one on the right and one on the left. And those who passed by derided him, wagging their heads and saying, "You who would destroy the temple and rebuild it in three days, save yourself! If you are the Son of God, come down from the cross." So also the chief priests, with the scribes and elders, mocked him, saying, "He saved others; he cannot save himself. He is the King of Israel; let him come down now from the cross, and we will believe in him. He trusts in God; let God deliver him now, if he desires him. For he said, 'I am the Son of God.' " And the robbers who were crucified with him also reviled him in the same way.

MATTHEW 27:35-44

We read that Jesus was offered "wine to drink, mixed with gall" (Matthew 27:34, NIV). This may have been either a mild poison to mercifully shorten the time of suffering or an opiate to ease pain. Either way, after getting a taste, he refused to drink it.

Pontius Pilate ordered that a placard be affixed to Jesus's cross. It read: "Jesus of Nazareth, the King of the Jews" (John 19:19). When the Jewish leaders objected, Pilate famously replied: "What I have written I have written" (John 19:22). ∎

Above: *Jesus on the Cross* by Anthony van Dyck (1599–1641).

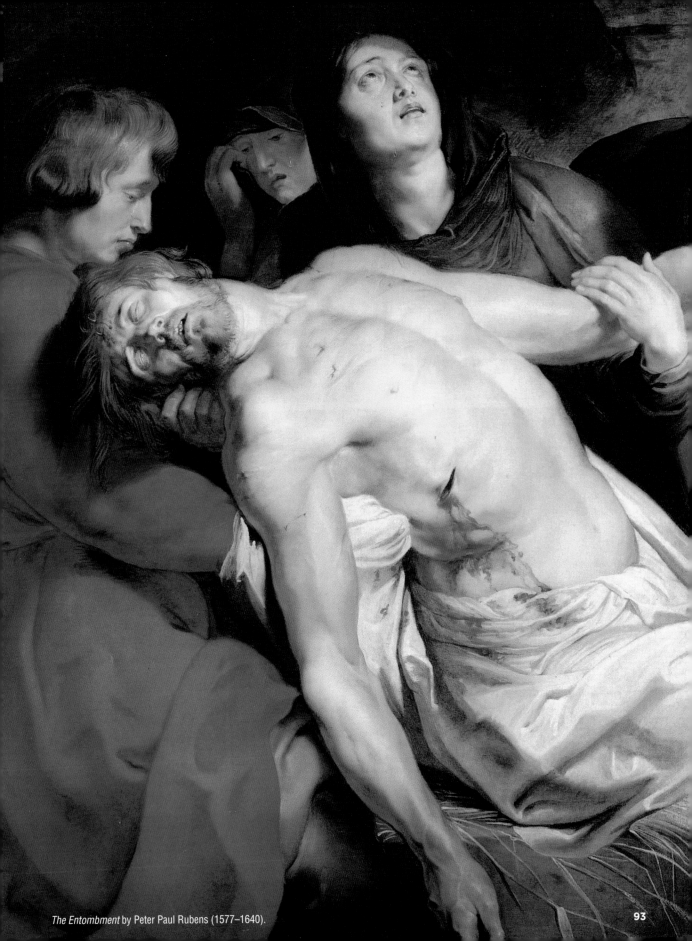

The Entombment by Peter Paul Rubens (1577–1640).

81 The Spear of Longinus

In a back corridor of Jerusalem's ancient Church of the Holy Sepulchre is a small shrine overlooked by most tourists. The shrine is dedicated to Longinus, the Roman soldier who, according to tradition, pierced Jesus's side while he hung on the cross (see John 19:34).

The spear of Longinus has fascinated people since the early days of the church. Ancient legends said that whoever acquires the spear controls the destiny of the world—and whoever loses possession of it forfeits their life. The spear was credited for the Roman emperor Constantine's ascension to power. Centuries later it was believed to have been in the possession of Charlemagne, ruler of the Holy Roman Empire. It is said that both men died shortly after losing possession of the spear.

A relic that resides in the Hofburg Museum in Vienna, Austria, is believed by some people to be the lance of Longinus. A legend is told that in the early twentieth century an unknown artist named Adolf Hitler spent hours at the museum staring at the spear.

According to the legend, many years later, when his Third Reich annexed Austria, Hitler wasted no time in seizing this artifact. In the final days of World War II, as the Allied armies were sweeping across Germany, the spear was discovered hidden in a deep cave. Ironically, hours later, Adolf Hitler was dead. ■

Above: *Jesus's Side Pierced by a Lance* by Fra Angelico (1395–1455).

82 The Site of Jesus's Tomb

Two competing sites in Jerusalem have been hailed as the tomb of Jesus. The first of these is located near a prominent outcropping of rock that resembles a skull, and which is thought to be Golgotha ("the place of a skull")—the site of the crucifixion.

Excavations at this prominent rocky crag situated just outside the city walls date to the sixteenth century and led to the discovery of a rock-cut tomb.

Although popular as a lovely setting in which to contemplate the death and resurrection of Jesus, the tomb has been found to be part of a complex dating from the Iron Age (late eighth to seventh century BC). As such, it could hardly be the "new tomb" belonging to Joseph of Arimathea (Matthew 27:60).

The second proposed site of Jesus's tomb is the Church of the Holy Sepulchre. Although inside the present-day city walls, the site was outside the city walls of Jesus's day and is built over an ancient tomb.

In the second century AD, the Roman emperor Hadrian unwittingly preserved the location of Jesus's tomb. Determined to erase all places of Jewish and Christian worship, he covered the tomb of Jesus with a massive pagan temple. This temple marked the site of Jesus's crucifixion for Emperor Constantine, who in the fourth century replaced the temple with the Church of the Holy Sepulchre. ■

Top: Dome of the Church of the Holy Sepulchre in the Old City of Jerusalem.
Right: A man prays near the Stone of Anointing in the Church of the Holy Sepulchre.

83

The Burial Cloth of Jesus

The Gospel of Mark states: "Joseph bought a long sheet of linen cloth. Then he took Jesus' body down from the cross, wrapped it in the cloth, and laid it in a tomb that had been carved out of the rock" (15:46, NLT).

Do we still have this linen cloth—the actual burial cloth of Jesus? Some say we do.

The famous fabric known as the Shroud of Turin is traceable to fourteenth-century France. Believers in its authenticity claim it is the same burial cloth that was venerated by the faithful in ancient times. They say it was brought to Europe in the Middle Ages.

In 1978 the Shroud of Turin Research Project brought together dozens of international scientists who studied the cloth. These experts were divided as to the artifact's genuineness. Some evidence seems to link the shroud to Israel. For example, embedded in the fabric are pollen spores native to historical Palestine. Also found were particles of an unusual form of limestone that is common in the hill country around Jerusalem.

The question of the shroud's age appeared to have been conclusively answered in 1988, when three separate laboratories dated it to between 1260 and 1390. Critics of this finding were quick to point out that water damage and fire may have distorted the results of the carbon dating. Other tests that use sophisticated infrared light technology have suggested fibers from the cloth may date between 300 BC and AD 400.

Perhaps the greatest mystery surrounding the Shroud of Turin is the bloodstained image imprinted on the cloth. Even cynics agree it does appear to be the likeness of a crucified man.

Many hope that future scientific advancements will one day definitively answer these lingering questions. ∎

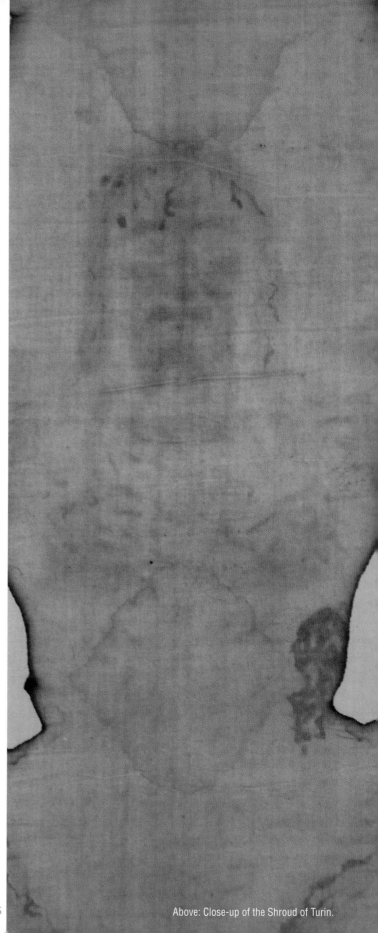

Above: Close-up of the Shroud of Turin.

CHAPTER SEVENTEEN

The Early Church

Painting depicting Pentecost from a church in Antwerp, Belgium.

84 The Fates of Jesus's Disciples

Jesus handpicked twelve of his followers to become the first apostles. Following the defection and suicide of Judas, Matthias was selected to take his place (Acts 1:26). By and large these men were unlikely candidates for the task of proclaiming the teachings of Jesus to the world. They lacked the formal training Jewish religious leaders typically underwent.

Over time others joined the ranks of Jesus's followers and became known as apostles, including the apostle Paul (formerly known as Saul). Acts 9 tells the story of his conversion. As a young man, he had been a student of the renowned rabbi Gamaliel (Acts 22:3), meaning he—unlike most of the other apostles—was the recipient of a world-class religious education. He later described his spiritual heritage: "circumcised on the eighth day, of the people of Israel, of the tribe of Benjamin, a Hebrew of Hebrews; in regard to the law, a Pharisee; as for zeal, persecuting the church" (Philippians 3:5–6, NIV).

"So one of the men who have accompanied us during all the time that the Lord Jesus went in and out among us, beginning from the baptism of John until the day when he was taken up from us—one of these men must become with us a witness to his resurrection." And they put forward two, Joseph called Barsabbas, who was also called Justus, and Matthias. And they prayed and said, "You, Lord, who know the hearts of all, show which one of these two you have chosen to take the place in this ministry and apostleship from which Judas turned aside to go to his own place." And they cast lots for them, and the lot fell on Matthias, and he was numbered with the eleven apostles.

ACTS 1:21–26

Probably due to his history as being an enemy of the followers of Jesus, Paul referred to himself as "the least of the apostles" (1 Corinthians 15:9).

What happened to all these men? James, the son of Zebedee, was executed by Herod Agrippa in approximately AD 44 (Acts 12:2). Christian historians calculate the martyrdom of Peter and Paul as taking place around AD 66.

According to tradition, the other apostles journeyed to far-flung lands, where they ministered fearlessly. Andrew was said to have preached in what is now Turkey, while "doubting" Thomas traveled eastward and is now regarded as the patron saint of India.

Philip, Matthew, and Bartholomew are believed to have found their way to Africa, while Matthias and James the son of Alphaeus reportedly evangelized in Syria. Simon the Zealot is thought to have preached in Persia.

Only John, who was exiled to the island of Patmos, is believed to have escaped martyrdom. ■

Above: *The Synaxis of the Twelve Apostles*, Moscow Museum.

Above: *The Crucifixion of Saint Peter* (1600–1601), Caravaggio.

85 Paul and the Mysteries of Tarsus

Tarsus was an important Mediterranean port city and the capital of the Roman province of Cilicia in what today is the nation of Turkey. With its dizzying array of philosophies, Tarsus was like "Athens East." It was also a hotbed for Greco-Roman mystery religions.

These secretive cults thrived on covert rituals and bizarre ceremonies known only to the "initiates." Their esoteric teachings, kept from the public, were thought to confer salvation upon the members of the cult—and exclude all others.

These facts make Paul's appeal to the commander of the Roman garrison in Jerusalem especially noteworthy: "I am a Jew of Tarsus in Cilicia, a citizen of no insignificant city; and I beg you, allow me to speak to the people" (Acts 21:39, NASB).

Paul's background granted him the knowledge to be able to point out the stark contrasts between the exclusiveness and secrecy of these mystery religions and the universal message he preached. Recorded in the Epistle to the Romans are the following words: "According to the revelation of the mystery which has been kept secret for long ages past, but now is manifested, and by the Scriptures of the prophets, according to the commandment of the eternal God, has been made known to all the nations, leading to obedience of faith; to the only wise God, through Jesus Christ" (Romans 16:25–27, NASB). ∎

86 Where Satan's Throne Is

The author of the book of Revelation addresses the church in Pergamum, repeating words he claimed were given to him by an angel: "I know where you dwell, where Satan's throne is. Yet you hold fast my name, and you did not deny my faith even in the days of Antipas my faithful witness, who was killed among you, where Satan dwells" (2:13).

Many suspect this is a reference to Antipas, bishop of Pergamum, during the persecution of Christians under the emperor Domitian (AD 81–96). According to tradition, Antipas was killed when he (a) would not cease preaching; and (b) refused to offer sacrifices to pagan idols. He was burned alive on a bull-shaped bronze altar that had been heated until it was red-hot.

This altar was located at the top of a stone staircase on the acropolis at Pergamum. It was part of a temple dedicated to either Zeus or Athena (or both), who were gods of the Greeks. A German archaeologist, Carl Humann, uncovered the altar in the 1860s and brought it piece by piece to Berlin, where it was eventually put on display in 1930.

Intrigued by this altar, Adolf Hitler is said to have used it as inspiration for the massive podium that was the centerpiece for his Nuremburg rallies. There, on the heights of a platform designed to look like the altar that originally stood "where Satan's throne is," the Fuhrer addressed his vast audiences of the Nazi party faithful. ∎

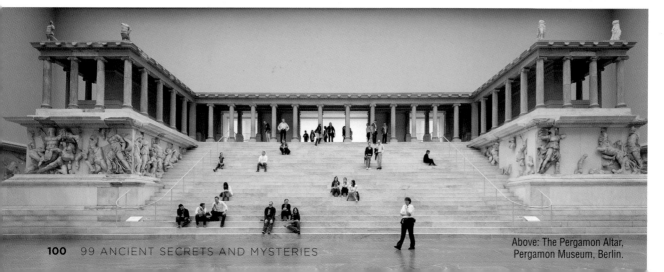

Above: The Pergamon Altar, Pergamon Museum, Berlin.

87 To an Unknown God

According to the book of Acts, Paul traveled to Athens, the cultural center of the ancient world, during his second missionary journey. He preached in the synagogue and later addressed a crowd in the marketplace, which was filled with temples and idols.

Paul's message intrigued a group of philosophers enough that they invited him to the Areopagus (sometimes called "Mars Hill"), a rocky height where "all the Athenians and the foreigners who lived there would spend their time in nothing except telling or hearing something new" (Acts 17:21).

Paul began by referring to what he had noticed in the city: "For as I passed along and observed the objects of your worship, I found also an altar with this inscription: 'To the unknown god.' What therefore you worship as unknown, this I proclaim to you" (Acts 17:23).

Why this odd inscription? The Greeks were polytheistic—meaning they believed in multiple gods. As such, the Athenians wanted to be careful that their religious observances did not inadvertently overlook—and possibly offend—some deity. We might call this their "catchall" or "just in case" altar. Writing 200 years later, the Greek biographer Diogenes Laërtius mentioned a plague, after which the populace of Athens was advised to sacrifice to the unknown god responsible for the epidemic.

Paul saw this inscription as his opportunity to introduce his Athenian listeners to "the God who made the world and everything in it, being Lord of heaven and earth" (Acts 17:24). ■

88 A Thorn in the Flesh

In the New Testament letter known as 2 Corinthians, we find a startling statement from the apostle Paul: "Therefore, in order to keep me from becoming conceited, I was given a thorn in my flesh, a messenger of Satan, to torment me. Three times I pleaded with the Lord to take it away from me. But he said to me, 'My grace is sufficient for you, for my power is made perfect in weakness'" (2 Corinthians 12:7–9, NIV).

Some people, who base their view on verses in the Hebrew Bible that compare wicked people to "thorns" (Isaiah 33:12; Nahum 1:10), have suggested Paul's mention of "a thorn in [his] flesh" refers to those who opposed his message. Others wonder if Paul was suffering from lingering guilt over the sins of his past,

which included persecuting the early Christians.

Most commentators look to subtle clues in the apostle's writings and suggest that some kind of physical ailment is in view. Did Paul perhaps suffer from a disease that affected his eyesight? In Galatians we read,, "For I testify to you that, if possible, you would have gouged out your eyes and given them to me" (4:15). Two chapters later he writes, "See with what large letters I am writing to you with my own hand" (6:11). Some Bible readers see these comments as referring to his poor vision.

Whatever this mysterious "thorn," Paul was somehow able to endure it—and many other forms of suffering (2 Corinthians 11:16–33)—while he tirelessly traveled, preached, and wrote. ■

Above Right: The Areopagus, Athens, Greece.   Below: *Paul the Apostle* (ca. 1657) by Rembrandt (1606–1669).

89 The Destruction of the Temple

In the Gospels we read about Jesus's prediction of the Jewish temple's destruction. Shortly before his death, Jesus was leaving the temple in Jerusalem. When one of his disciples exclaimed, " 'Look, Teacher, what large stones and what large buildings!' Jesus responded, 'Do you see these great buildings? Not one stone will be left here upon another; all will be thrown down' " (Mark 13:1–2, NRSV).

This was the Second Temple, built by Zerubbabel and the other Jewish exiles returning from Babylon, beginning in 516 BC. It had been refurbished and enlarged on a grand scale by Herod the Great and was the pride of the Jewish people.

In AD 70, the Romans conquered Jerusalem during the First Jewish Revolt. Against the orders of their commander, Titus, overzealous soldiers set the temple on fire, which resulted in its complete destruction.

Most of the collapsed edifice has long since disappeared, but part of its underlying retaining wall is still visible and yields important clues as to what happened to the structure above it.

The retaining wall is built from beautifully trimmed stones with beveled edges, many weighing up to fifty tons. The outer face was perfectly joined without the use of mortar. Knowing that limestone expands as it absorbs water, the building's engineers were careful to leave space for expansion behind the facade.

Forensic study of these remains suggests that when the temple was set afire, the superheated moisture could not escape. This caused the blocks to explode, collapsing the walls of the temple—and seeming to confirm the prophecy of Jesus. ∎

Top: *The Siege and Destruction of Jerusalem by the Romans under the Command of Titus, AD 70* (1850) by David Roberts (1796–1864).
Bottom: Jewish man praying at the Western Wall in Jerusalem.

CHAPTER EIGHTEEN

The Culmination of All Things

The Lamb of God, fresco by Friedrich Stummel (1850–1919) and Karl Wenzel (1887–1947), Herz Jesu Church, Berlin.

90 The Last Days

According to the Gospels, just a few days before his death, Jesus sat on the Mount of Olives, east of Jerusalem, talking of events leading up to "the end of the age" (Matthew 24:3). Jesus warned of "wars and rumors of wars . . . famines and earthquakes in various places" (Matthew 24:6–7). As he spoke, his followers peppered him with questions. The book of Luke reports Jesus's dire prediction that Jerusalem would be destroyed, "trampled underfoot by the Gentiles, until the times of the Gentiles are fulfilled" (Luke 21:24).

Later, other New Testament writers reflected on events of Jesus's return and the last days (see, Acts 2:17; 1 Thessalonians 4:16–18; 1 Peter 4:7). It's no wonder, then, that for over nineteen centuries people have continued to puzzle over these passages in the Bible and ask, "Are these the last days of human history?"

The Bible doesn't offer a clear answer or an exact date for the end of the age. As Jesus spoke about "the kingdom of God" (Luke 4:43), which some people believe will bring an end to wickedness and make the earth a paradise, inquisitive people wanted to know when the kingdom would come. To those who wanted to know details about Jesus's second coming, Jesus's answer adds to the mystery, "But concerning that day and hour no one knows, not even the angels of heaven, nor the Son, but the Father only" (Matthew 24:36). ■

Above: *The Fourth Horseman, Death on the Pale Horse* (1865) by Gustave Doré (1832–1883).

91 Who Are the 144,000 Witnesses?

Of all the biblical books of prophecy, perhaps none are more scrutinized and debated than the New Testament book of Revelation. This end-times vision, written by John near the end of the first century, overflows with vivid images and puzzling statements. One reason to feel puzzled is we have no context for some of the events mentioned.

One such passage is Revelation 7:3–4. It depicts servants of God receiving some sort of seal on their foreheads. The text says, "One hundred and forty-four thousand of all the tribes of the children of Israel were sealed" (Revelation 7:4, NKJV).

The exact nature of this "seal" is not specified, although in ancient times seals signified security or protection (Matthew 27:66), or they indicated ownership (Ephesians 1:13). The number 144,000 has also intrigued Bible readers.

Many view the number as a symbolic reference to all those in the last days who will faithfully endure a "great tribulation" (Revelation 7:14).

Others believe this to be a literal prophecy that 12,000 members from each of Israel's twelve tribes will become adherents of Christianity. This view is challenged by those who point out that following the Assyrian invasion in 722 BC, the Babylonian exile between 605 and 586 BC, and the fall of Jerusalem and diaspora of the Jews in AD 70, any talk of distinctive Jewish tribes is essentially meaningless.

Whether literal or figurative, the number 144,000 and its impact are shown to be significant in the book of Revelation. John reported seeing in heaven, as a result of the witness of the 144,000 people, "a great multitude that no one could number, from every nation, from all tribes and peoples and languages, standing before the throne and before the Lamb" (Revelation 7:9). ∎

And I heard the number of the sealed, 144,000, sealed from every tribe of the sons of Israel . . . . After this I looked, and behold, a great multitude that no one could number, from every nation, from all tribes and peoples and languages, standing before the throne and before the Lamb, clothed in white robes, with palm branches in their hands, and crying out with a loud voice, "Salvation belongs to our God who sits on the throne, and to the Lamb!"

REVELATION 7:4, 9–10

Above: *Christ Glorified in the Court of Heaven* (detail) by Fra Angelico (1395–1455).

92 666: The Number of the Beast

The book of Revelation refers repeatedly to a mysterious figure known as "the beast." It is described as ascending "from the bottomless pit" (11:7). Elsewhere it is shown "rising out of the sea, with ten horns and seven heads" (13:1).

Is this "beast" a single, powerful leader who will lead the whole world astray? Is this image suggestive of a global political system that opposes God and his purposes? People, as you might imagine, have all sorts of theories.

The most famous clue as to the identity of the beast is this cryptic statement: "This calls for wisdom: let the one who has understanding calculate the number of the beast, for it is the number of a man, and his number is 666" (Revelation 13:18).

What's the significance of this infamous number, 666?[1]

Many Bible scholars suggest that numbers are often used symbolically in the Bible. For example, they claim that the number seven symbolizes perfection or completeness because God rested on the seventh day of creation (Genesis 2:2–3) and proclaimed the Sabbath as a day of rest for the people of Israel (Deuteronomy 5:12). Some Bible scholars go as far as saying that six, being one less than seven, seems to represent imperfection (1 Chronicles 20:6; Daniel 3:1).

Some have turned to *gematria* for answers. Gematria is the ancient practice of assigning numerical values to letters—almost a form of code. By this system, people look for hidden meanings in words or numbers. Using gematria, some have claimed that 666 is the numerical equivalent of *Nero*, the name of the Roman emperor and the first great persecutor of the church. This kind of speculation makes for interesting discussions; but in truth, there is not enough evidence to claim with any certainty that the author of Revelation was employing a hidden biblical code in this, or any other, verse. ■

[1] There are two textual variants to the number 666. One is 616 (from P115, 3rd century, and Codex C, 5th century); the other is 665 (from ms 2344, 11th century).

Top: Bust of Nero at the Capitoline Museum, Rome.
Below: *Nero's Torches* (1876) by Henryk Siemiradzki (1843–1902).

93 The Identity of Babylon the Great

In Genesis, the first book of the Bible, we read about Babel in the story where God thwarts a human attempt to build a city with a great tower (Genesis 11). Babel eventually became Babylon, the capital city of the dominant world empire of the seventh and sixth centuries BC. In the Hebrew Bible, the Babylonians are one of Israel's most feared enemies.

In the last book of the Bible, we read about "Babylon the great" (Revelation 14:8, 18:2). But instead of descriptions of an ancient metropolis, we are treated to a wild, apocalyptic image: a bejeweled woman, called a harlot, riding a scarlet beast with seven heads. The woman is said to be drunk from killing followers of God. She holds a big golden cup full of nasty things.

Some speculate that John's description of a beast with "seven heads [that] are seven mountains" (Revelation 17:9) could be a reference to Rome, the city of seven hills. Other suggestions include the European Economic Community, the United States, and even the city of Babylon itself in Iraq. They note that Revelation describes the beast and its rider as a great economic power whose destruction causes great distress: "And the merchants of the earth weep and mourn for her, since no one buys their cargo anymore" (Revelation 18:11).

While the meaning of "Babylon the great" remains a mystery, many people devoted to biblical prophecy believe that in due time the identity of the beast and its evil rider will surely be revealed. ∎

Top: Restored ruins of ancient Babylon, Iraq.
Left: *The Whore of Babylon* (1523) by Hans Burgkmair (1473–1531).

94 Is America in Bible Prophecy?

Though we find overt references to various modern-day nations—Egypt, Ethiopia, Syria, Libya—in the prophetic portions of the Bible, we don't see explicit mentions of the United States.

This prompts some Bible readers to ask, "Does this mean America will no longer be a recognized nation in the last days? Or do the ancient biblical writings refer to the United States by some other name?"

Some think they see a potential allusion to America in this phrase from Ezekiel 38:13: "the merchants of Tarshish, and all their young lions" (NKJV).

Could the merchants of Tarshish, they ask, refer to those living in Tartessos (Tartessus), the ancient city-state on the southwest coast of what today is the nation of Spain? It was, after all, from ports in this region that Christopher Columbus set sail for the New World. Also, Franciscan missionaries embarking from this area brought the Christian religion to the native peoples of the Americas.

Others speculate that since the lion is the national emblem of Great Britain, Ezekiel's "young lions" reference could possibly refer to the future United States colonies.

Is this sort of thinking careful scholarship or the product of an overactive imagination? You be the judge. ■

95 Armageddon: The Mount of Megiddo

Many people believe the Bible's references to a final cosmic battle between the forces of good and evil are meant to be interpreted symbolically. Others interpret them literally. They point to Revelation 16:16: "They assembled them at the place that in Hebrew is called Armageddon."

Armageddon is from the Hebrew words *Har Megiddo*, meaning "Mount of Megiddo." Tel Megiddo, in northern Israel, is an actual place. It features a hill—not a true mountain—that overlooks the Jezreel Valley where the Via Maris, a major route from Egypt to Mesopotamia, passes. Several important battles in biblical history took place at this site.

And yet other biblical prophecies of an epic end-times clash do not mention Armageddon. The book of Joel, for example, describes a showdown to the south, in a valley outside Jerusalem: "I will gather all nations and bring them down to the Valley of Jehoshaphat" (Joel 3:2, NIV).

Those expecting a literal battle argue that this seeming discrepancy can be explained by the tiny geographic boundaries of Israel. Since the combatants in this final showdown are said to be "all nations," a single battlefield could never contain that many warring troops. A conflict of that scale would inevitably spill across the land of Israel.

Did the writer of Revelation mean for us to expect earth's climactic battle at this site? The unfolding of this mystery remains to be seen! ■

Top: *Christopher Columbus Landing in the New World, 1492.*
Left: Jezreel Valley, taken from Megiddo/Armageddon Hill, Israel.

96 The Meaning of the Millennium

The word millennium is not found in most English translations of the Bible. It comes instead from the Latin words *mille* (which means "thousand") and *annus* ("year"). Some Bible readers and scholars use this word because of a phrase used near the end of the book of the Revelation. The passage describes a great angel on a heavenly mission: "He seized the dragon, that ancient serpent, who is the devil and Satan, and bound him for *a thousand years*" (20:2, emphasis added).

Some see this verse as John's way of saying, "Expect a literal, thousand-year period of peace and prosperity on the earth." Based on the verse that follows—"After that he must be released for a little while" (Revelation 20:3)—they further expect Satan to launch a final desperate battle against God after this thousand-year period.

And he seized the dragon, that ancient serpent, who is the devil and Satan, and bound him for a thousand years, and threw him into the pit, and shut it and sealed it over him, so that he might not deceive the nations any longer, until the thousand years were ended. After that he must be released for a little while.
REVELATION 20:2–3

Other Bible readers don't anticipate a literal millennium. They see the number "thousand" used in other biblical contexts merely to imply fullness or immensity (Deuteronomy 7:9; Psalms 50:10, 84:10). They therefore take this verse as John's way of saying, "We should expect an endless future of harmony and holiness under the Messiah's rule."

The absence of confirmation about the millennium from other end-times prophecy leaves many people to wonder in faith about the mystery of God's work through history. ■

97 All Eyes on the Books

The Hebrew prophet Daniel had a vision in which thousands were standing in a court where "books were opened" (Daniel 7:10). John, the author of Revelation, concludes the New Testament with a similar vision: "Then I saw a great white throne and him who was seated on it. The earth and the heavens fled from his presence, and there was no place for them. . . . The dead were judged according to what they had done as recorded in the books" (20:11–12, NIV).

What about these mysterious references to "books"? Most agree these "books" (divine records of the deeds of humanity), provide evidence to support a final judgment for each person.

Revelation also mentions a "book of life" (Revelation 20:12). Unlike the records of deeds, this book contains the eternal roster of heaven (Luke 10:20). Are these book references meant to be literal or symbolic? People who have faith in a promise of eternal life in heaven receive encouragement in believing their names will be found in this book of life on that final day of judgment. ■

Right: *Paradise* by Giusto de' Menabuoi (1320–1391).

The final chapters of the Bible reveal a prophetic picture of the eternal state: "I saw a new heaven and a new earth, for the first heaven and the first earth had passed away . . . And I saw the holy city, new Jerusalem, coming down out of heaven from God . . . And I heard a loud voice from the throne saying, 'Behold, the dwelling place of God is with man. He will dwell with them, and they will be his people, and God himself will be with them as their God' " (Revelation 21:1–3).

So much about this passage is mysterious.

In former times the presence of God was represented by the ark of the covenant or hidden in the inner Most Holy Place of the temple. In the new Jerusalem, God will openly rule over his people: "Behold, the dwelling place of God is with man. He will dwell with them, and they will be his people, and God himself will be with them as their God" (Revelation 21:3).

According to Revelation, the new Jerusalem will be the fulfillment of humankind's deepest aspirations: "He will wipe away every tear from their eyes, and death shall be no more, neither shall there be mourning, nor crying, nor pain anymore" (21:4).

The immense proportions of the city have led many commentators to suggest that it is a symbolic expression of the perfection and majesty of God. The materials used in its construction also defy imagination: pure gold, clear as glass, and an abundance of precious jewels.

If intended to be taken literally, the descriptions of this city hold great mystery for us. Truly a city of such proportions could only reflect a magnificence characteristic of its designer. ∎

The apostle Peter wrote of a day "in which the heavens will pass away with a great noise, and the elements will melt with fervent heat; both the earth and the works that are in it will be burned up" (2 Peter 3:10, NKJV). Some modern-day interpreters have wondered if this might be an ancient biblical description of global thermonuclear war. Others have argued that it would take more than human-made bombs to cause the "elements" to melt and the "heavens" to pass away.

Some scientists have speculated that perhaps our universe will collapse or collide with another. Astronomers believe for good reasons that our sun will eventually die.

The story of the Bible begins with a paradise that was lost and then describes the acts of God in human history that culminate in a world made new. It includes the apostle Paul's intriguing words about the dawn of a new age: "The creation itself will be set free from its bondage to corruption and obtain the freedom of the glory of the children of God. For we know that the whole creation has been groaning together in the pains of childbirth until now" (Romans 8:21–22).

What can we say? God's epoch-ending actions described in such Bible passages as these are as jaw-dropping as his work to create the universe "in the beginning" (Genesis 1:1). ■

Top: Eibsee, lake in the German Alps.
Left: The painting from the dome of the Abbey of Saint Gallen.

museum of the Bible

Experience the Book that Shapes History

Museum of the Bible is a 430,000-square-foot building located in the heart of Washington, D.C.—just steps from the National Mall and the U.S. Capitol. Displaying artifacts from several collections, the Museum explores the Bible's history, narrative and impact through high-tech exhibits, immersive settings, and interactive experiences. Upon entering, you pass through two massive, bronze gates resembling printing plates from Genesis 1. Beyond the gates, an incredible replica of an ancient artifact containing Psalm 19 hangs behind etched glass panels. Come be inspired by the imagination and innovation used to display thousands of years of biblical history.

Museum of the Bible aims to be the most technologically advanced museum in the world, starting with its unique Digital Guide that allows guests to personalize their museum experience with navigation, customized tours, supplemental visual and audio content, and more.

For more information and to plan your visit, go to museumoftheBible.org.